ACOUSTIC CHRISTIAN HITS

ISBN 978-1-4584-2142-5

HAL•LEONARD®
CORPORATION
7777 W. BLUEMOUND RD. P.O. BOX 13819 MILWAUKEE, WI 53213

For all works contained herein:
Unauthorized copying, arranging, adapting, recording, Internet posting, public performance,
or other distribution of the printed music in this publication is an infringement of copyright.
Infringers are liable under the law.

Visit Hal Leonard Online at
www.halleonard.com

CONTENTS

AMAZING GRACE
(My Chains Are Gone)

Words by JOHN NEWTON
Traditional American Melody
Additional Words and Music by CHRIS TOMLIN
and LOUIE GIGLIO

Gently

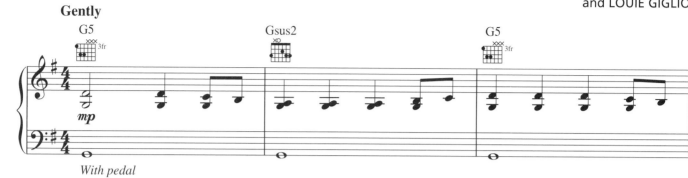

With pedal

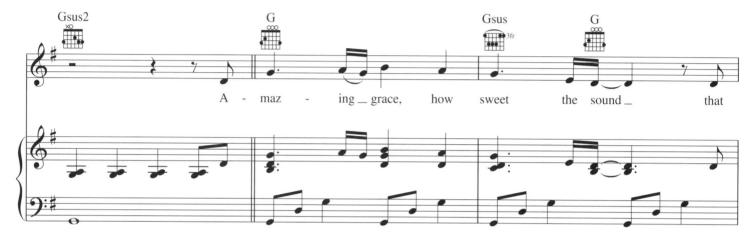

A - maz - ing _ grace, how sweet the sound _ that

saved a _ wretch like _ me. I _ once was lost but

now I'm found, was _ blind but now _____ I see. 'Twas

© 2006 WORSHIPTOGETHER.COM SONGS (ASCAP) and sixsteps Music (ASCAP)
Admin. at EMICMGPUBLISHING.COM
All Rights Reserved   Used by Permission

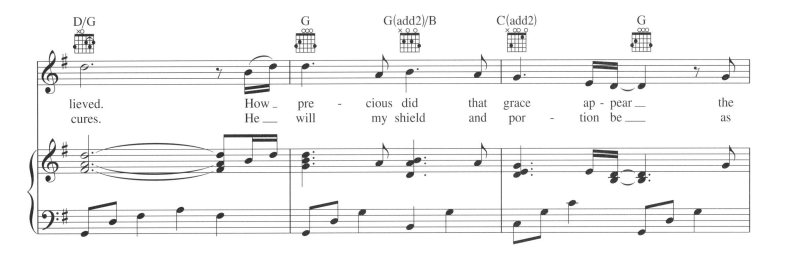

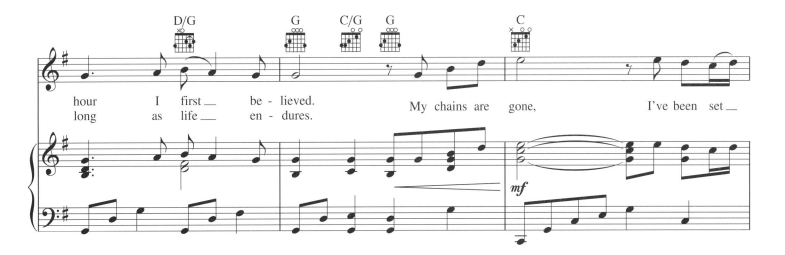

me. And like a ____ flood, _____ His mer - cy

rains un - end - ing love, a - maz - ing grace.

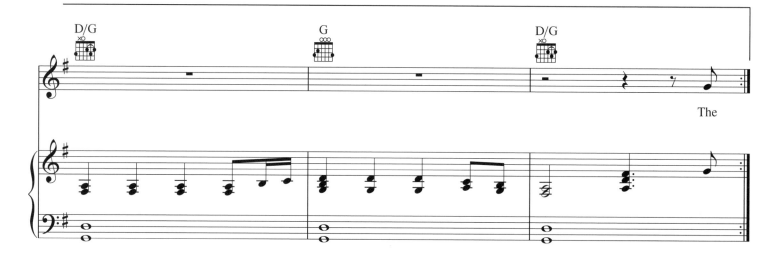

The

grace. My chains are gone, I've been set ___ free. My God, my

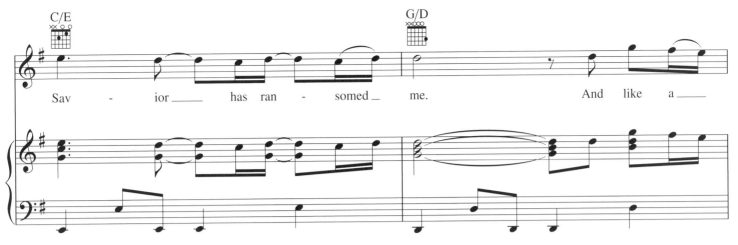

Sav - ior _____ has ran - somed _____ me. And like a _____

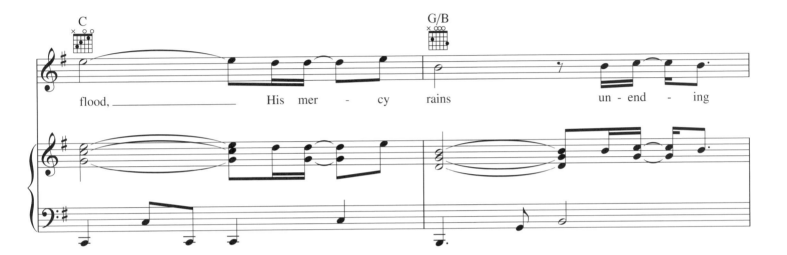

flood, _____ His mer - cy rains un - end - ing

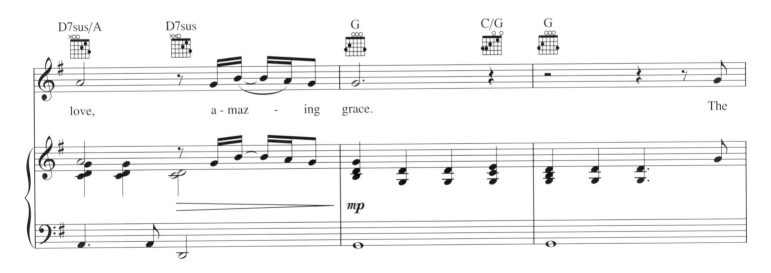

love, a - maz - ing grace. The

earth shall soon dis - solve like snow, the sun for - bear to

shine. But _ God, who _ called _____ me here be - low will

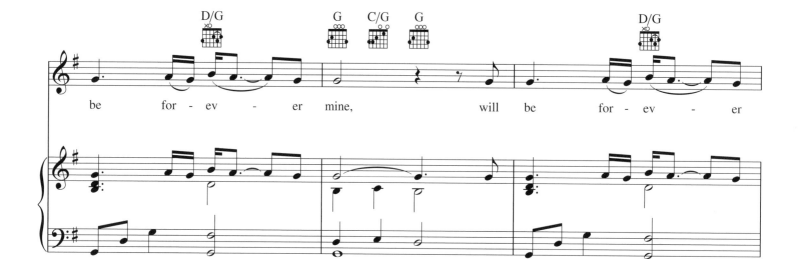

be for - ev - er mine, will be for - ev - er

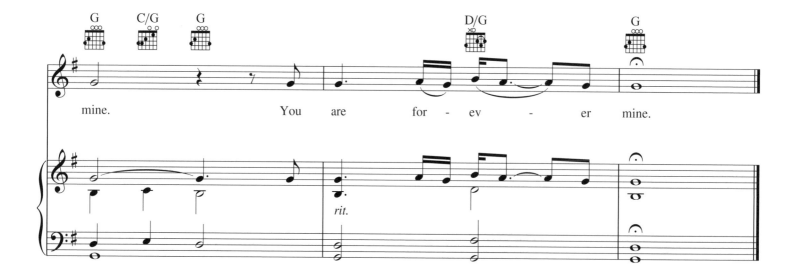

mine. You are for - ev - er mine.

BEAUTIFUL THINGS

Words and Music by MICHAEL GUNGOR
and LISA GUNGOR

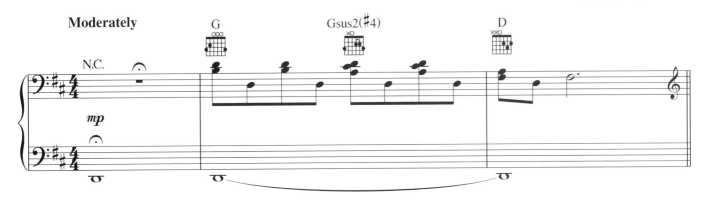

All this pain; ___ I won-der if I'll ev-er find my way. ___

___ I won-der if my life could real-ly change ___ at ___ all.

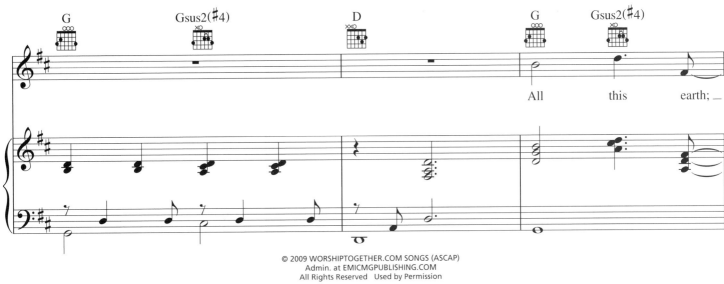

All this earth; ___

© 2009 WORSHIPTOGETHER.COM SONGS (ASCAP)
Admin. at EMICMGPUBLISHING.COM
All Rights Reserved   Used by Permission

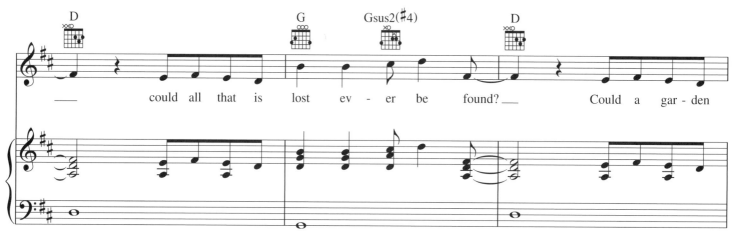

could all that is lost ev - er be found? ___ Could a gar - den

come up from this ground ___ at ___ all?

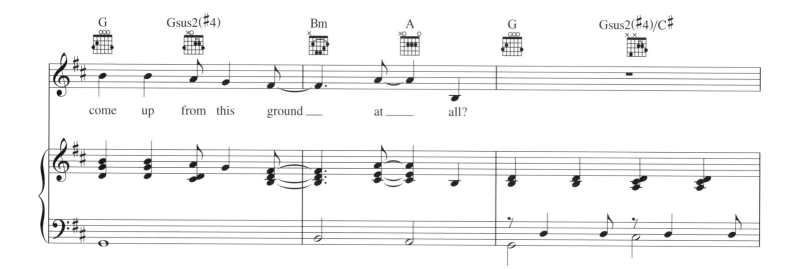

You make beau - ti - ful things, ___ You make ___ beau - ti -

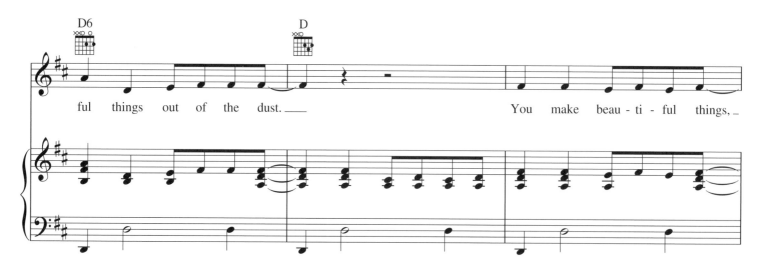

ful things out of the dust. ___ You make beau - ti - ful things, ___

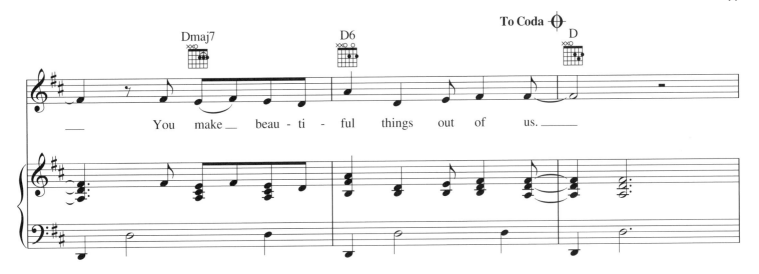

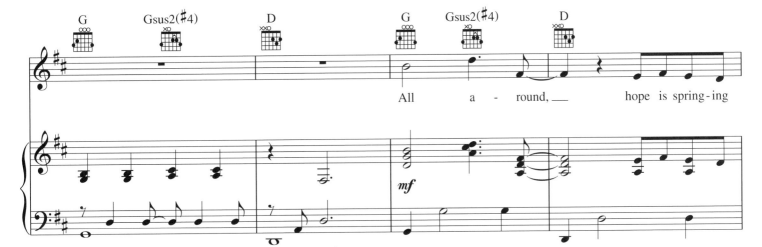

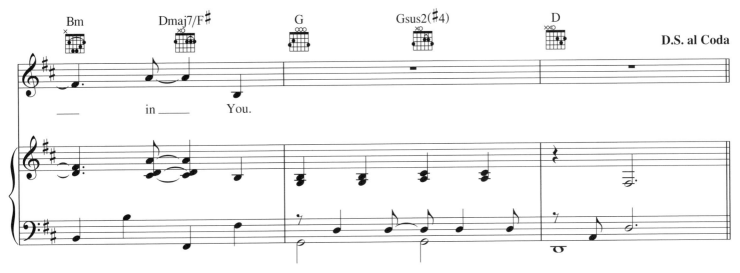

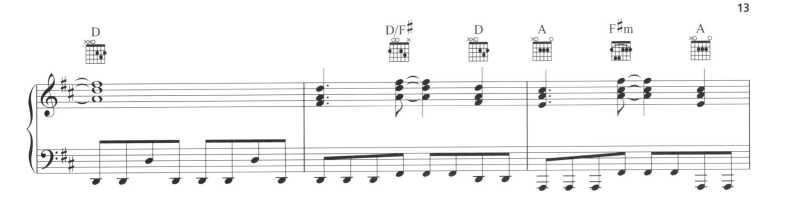

You make __ me new, You __ are

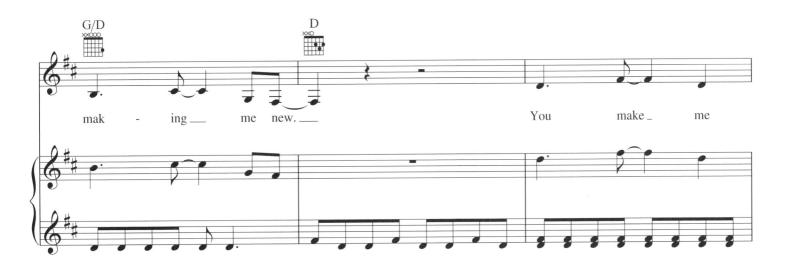

mak - ing __ me new. __ You make __ me

new, You __ are mak - ing __ me new. __ (Mak - ing me new.)

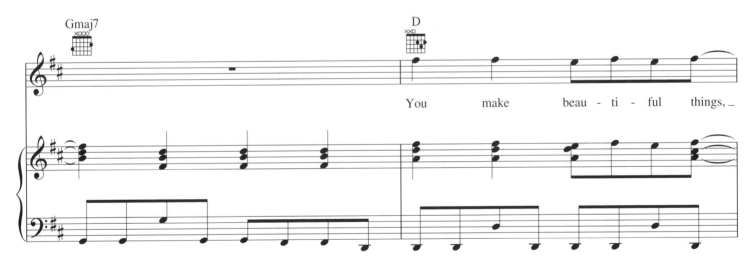

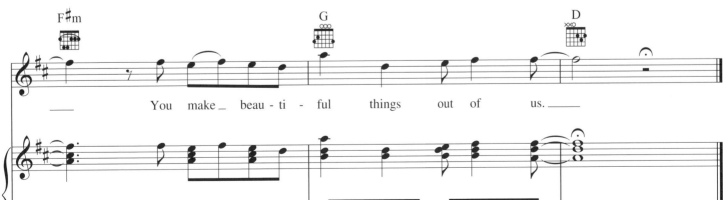

BLESSINGS

Words and Music by
LAURA MIXON STORY

Moderately slow, in 2

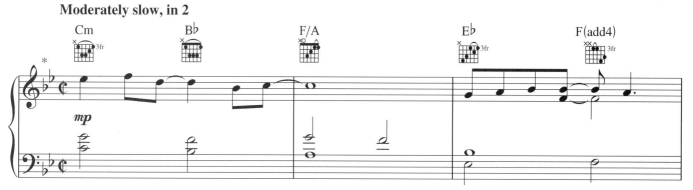

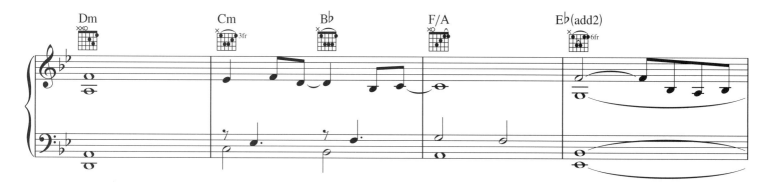

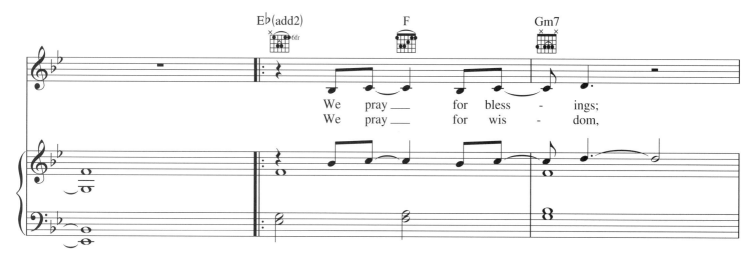

We pray ____ for bless - ings;
We pray ____ for wis - dom,

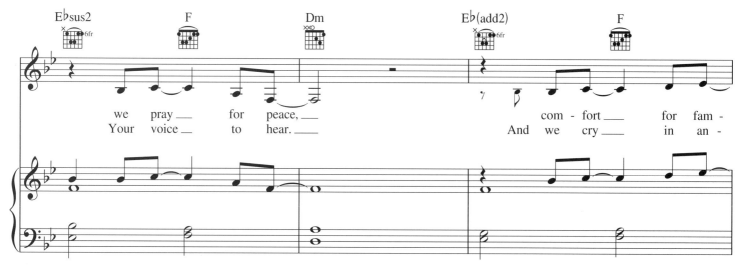

we pray ____ for peace, ____
Your voice ____ to hear. ____

com - fort ____ for fam -
And we cry ____ in an -

* Recorded a half step higher.

© 2011 New Spring Publishing (ASCAP) and Laura Stories (ASCAP)
All Rights Administered by New Spring Publishing
All Rights Reserved   Used by Permission

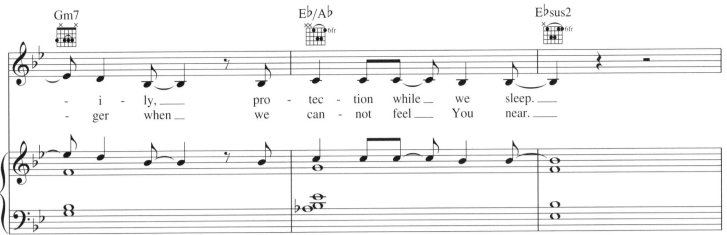

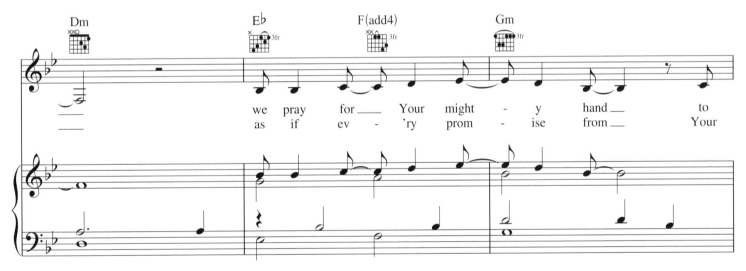

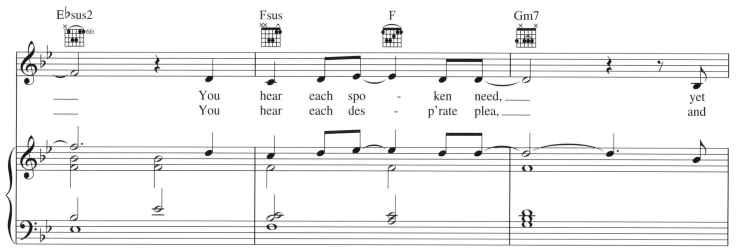

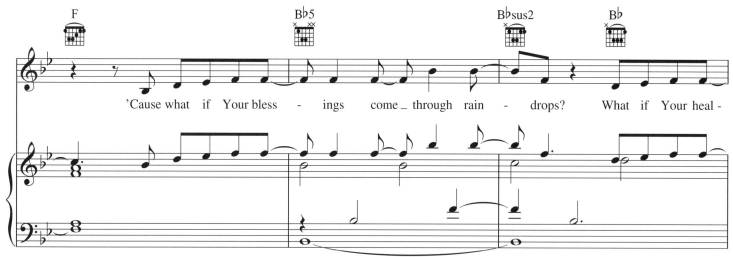

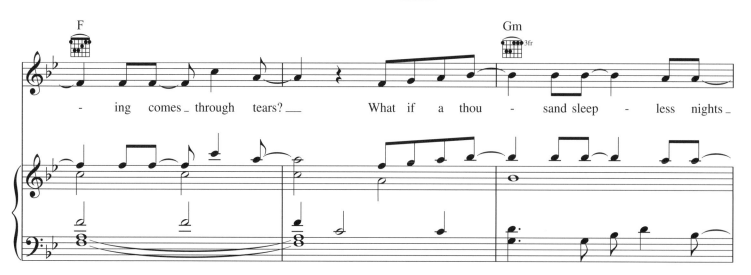

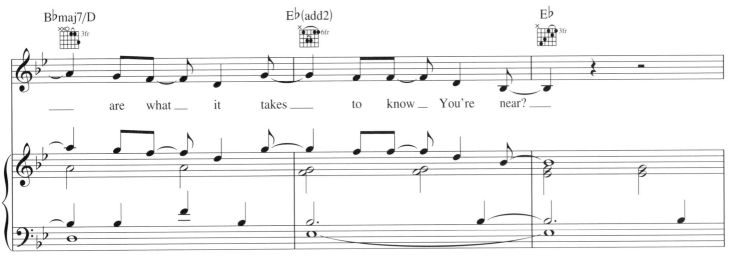

are what ___ it takes ___ to know ___ You're near? ___

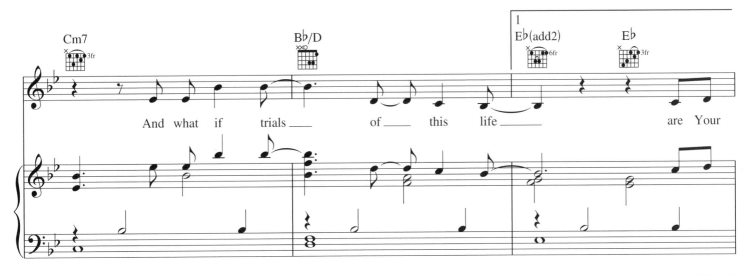

And what if trials ___ of ___ this life _____ are Your

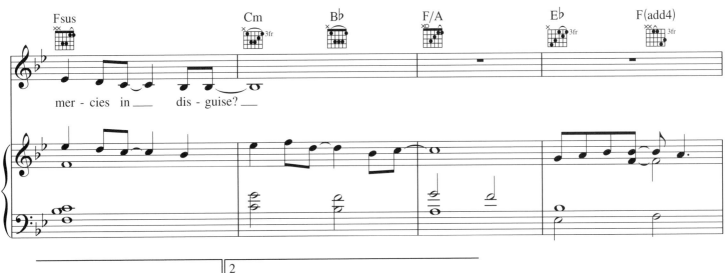

mer - cies in ___ dis - guise? ___

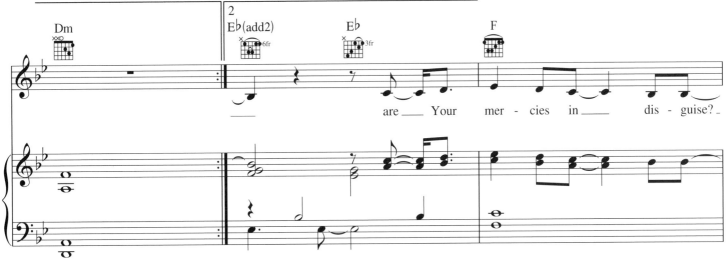

___ are ___ Your mer - cies in ___ dis - guise? ___

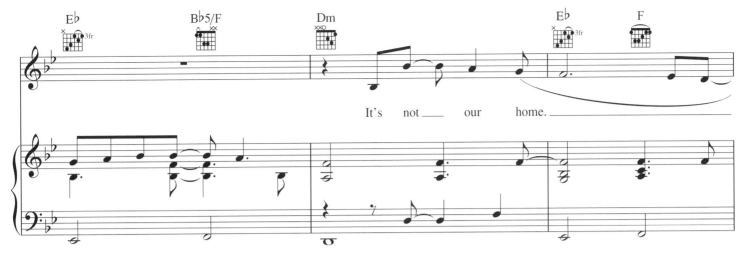

It's not ___ our home. ___

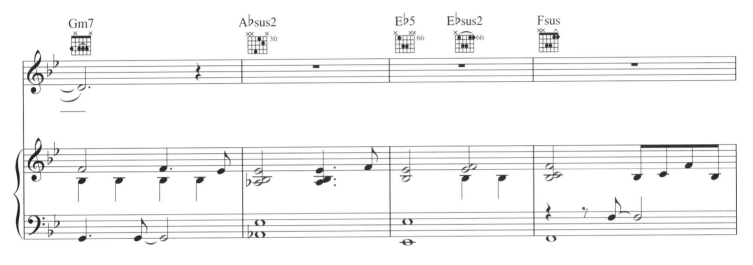

'Cause what if Your bless - ings come ___ through rain - drops? What if Your heal -

- ing comes ___ through tears? ___ And what if a thou - sand sleep - less nights ___

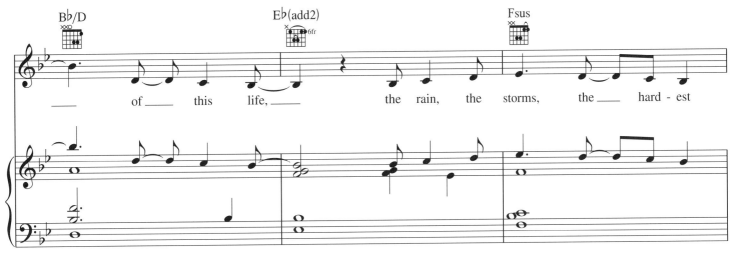

of ___ this life, ___ the rain, the storms, the ___ hard-est

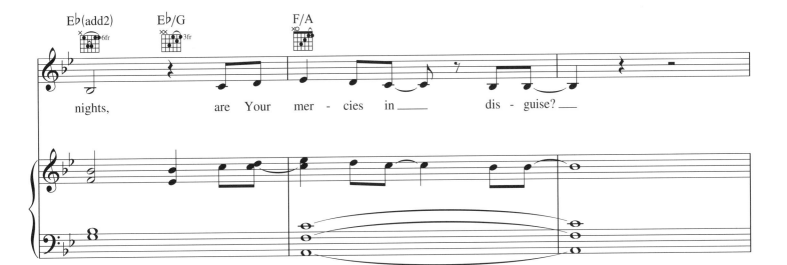

nights, are Your mer - cies in ___ dis - guise? ___

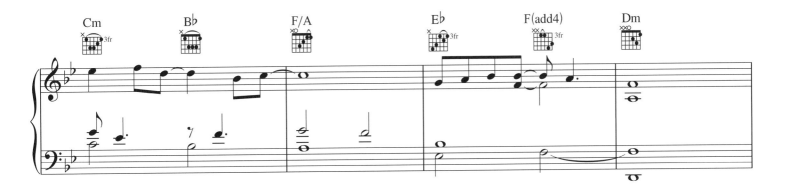

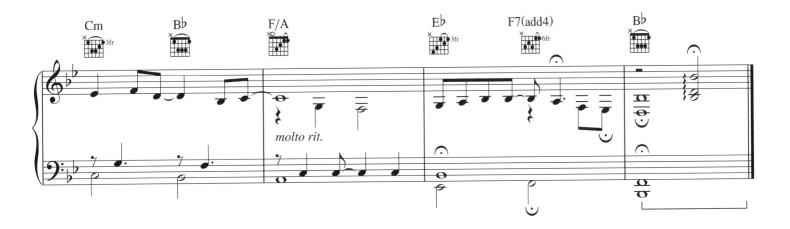

molto rit.

BY HIS WOUNDS

Words and Music by MAC POWELL
and DAVID NASSER

Gently

He was pierced for our ___ trans-gres-sions, He was crushed for ___ our sins. ___ The

© 2007 MEAUX MERCY (BMI), CONSUMING FIRE MUSIC (ASCAP) and REDEMPTIVE ART MUSIC (BMI)
Admin. at EMICMGPUBLISHING.COM
All Rights Reserved   Used by Permission

pun-ish-ment _ that brought _ us peace _ was up-on _ Him. _____ And

by His _ wounds, _____ by His _ wounds _ we are healed. _

He was

We are healed __ by _____ Your sac -

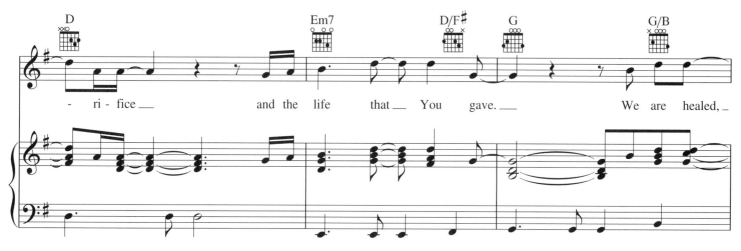

-ri - fice ___ and the life that ___ You gave. ___ We are healed, ___

___ for ___ You paid ___ the price. ___ By Your grace we ___ are saved, ___

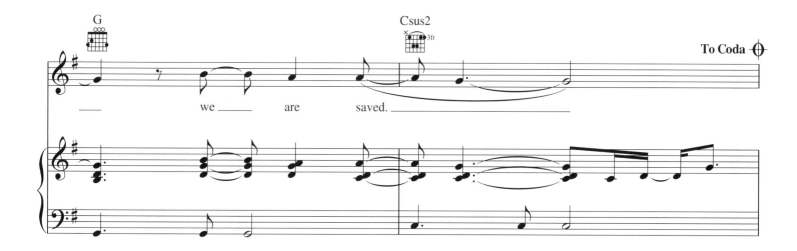

___ we ___ are saved. ___

To Coda

He was pierced for our ___ trans - gres - sions and

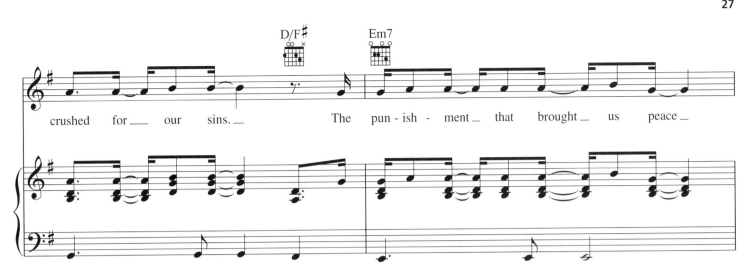

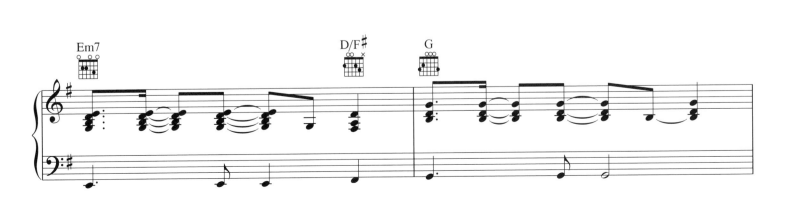

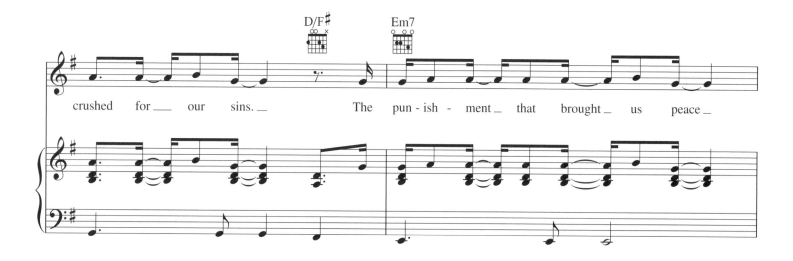

by His __ wounds __ we are healed. __

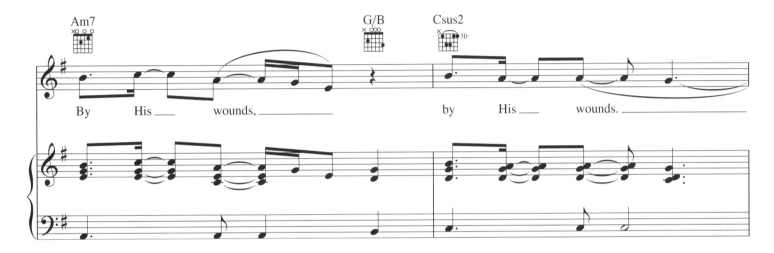

By His __ wounds, _____ by His __ wounds. _____

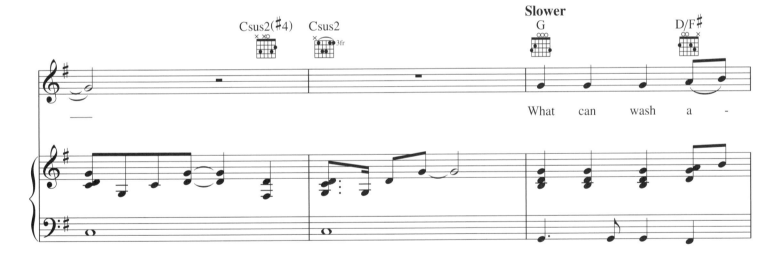

Slower

__ What can wash a -

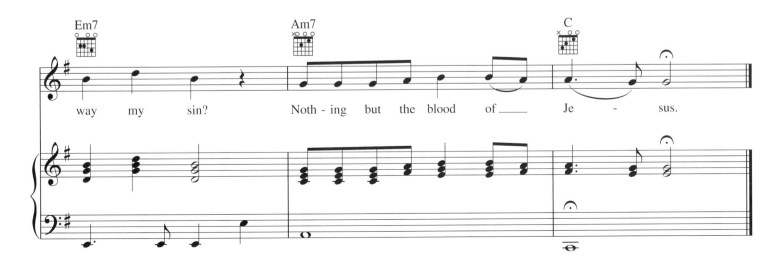

way my sin? Noth - ing but the blood of __ Je - sus.

FINALLY HOME

Words and Music by BART MILLARD,
BARRY GRAUL and MIKE SCHEUCHZER

Gently

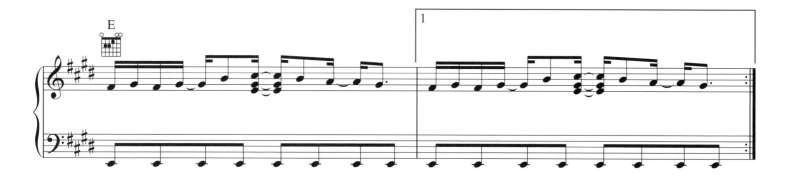

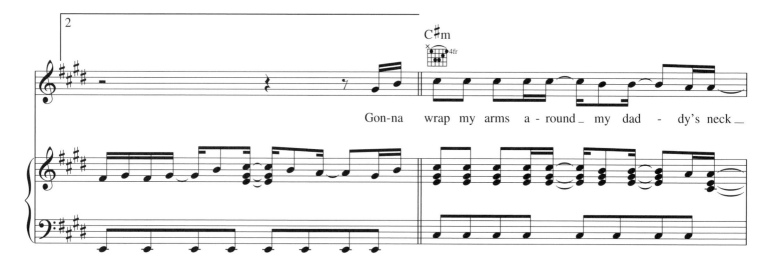

Gon-na wrap my arms a-round__ my dad - dy's neck__

___ and tell__ him that I've missed him. ___

© 2007 Simpleville Music and Wet As A Fish Music
All Rights Admin. by Simpleville Publishing, LLC
All Rights Reserved   Used by Permission

And tell him all a-bout _ the man _ that I _ be-came, _

_ and hope _ that it pleased him. _

There's so much _ I wan-na say, _ so much _

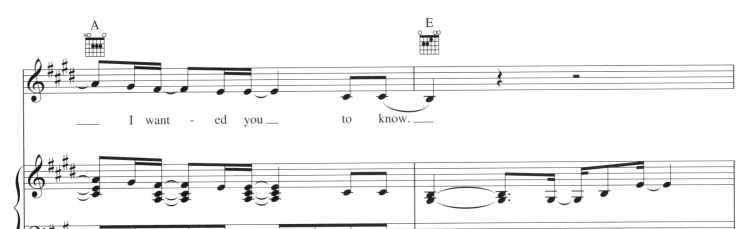

_ I want-ed you _ to know. _

When I fi - n'lly

make it home.

When I fi - n'lly

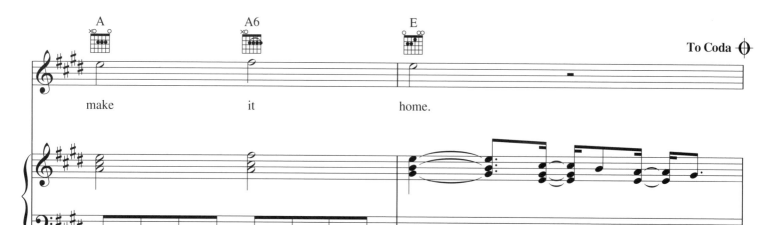

make it home.

Then I'll gaze up-on ___ the throne ___ of ___ the King, ___

___ fro - zen in my steps. ___

And all the ques-tions that ___ I ___ swore ___ I ___ would ask, ___

___ words ___ just won't come yet. ___

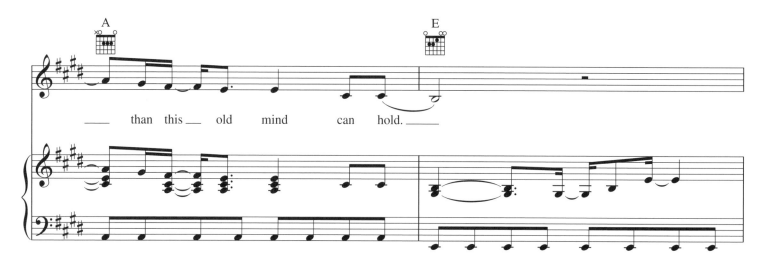

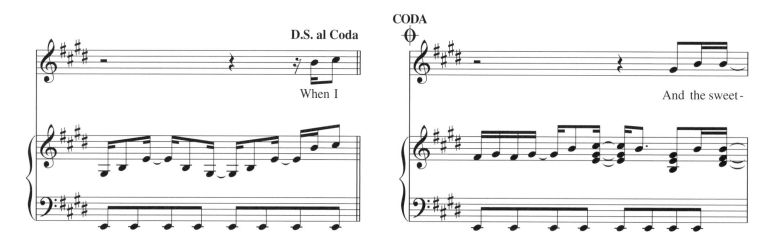

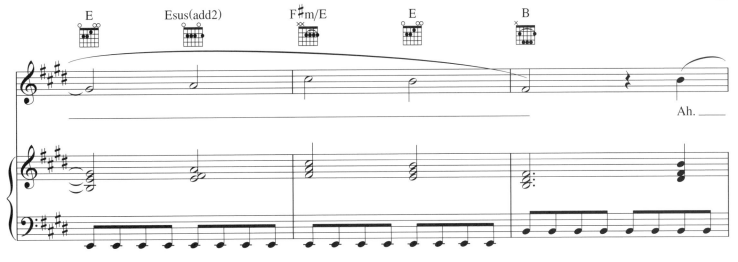

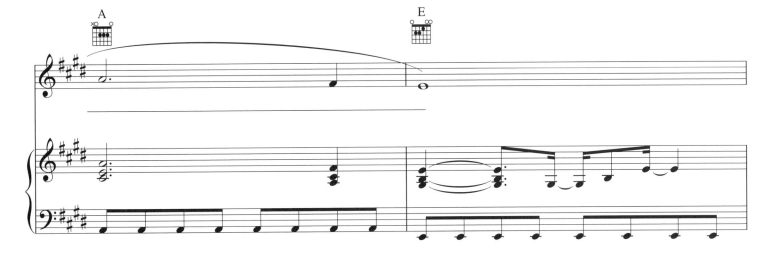

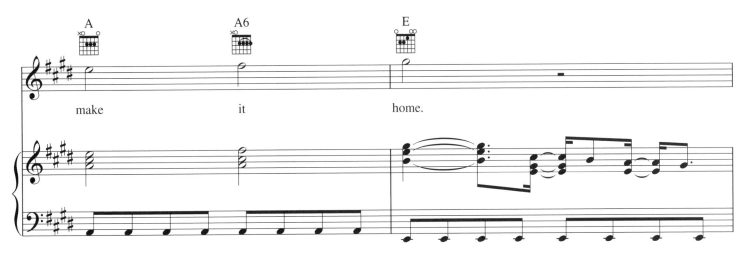

When I fi - n'lly

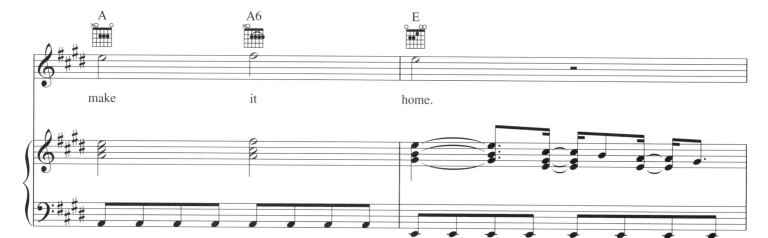

make it home.

Ooh. _____

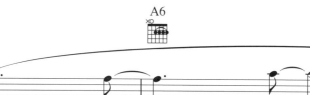

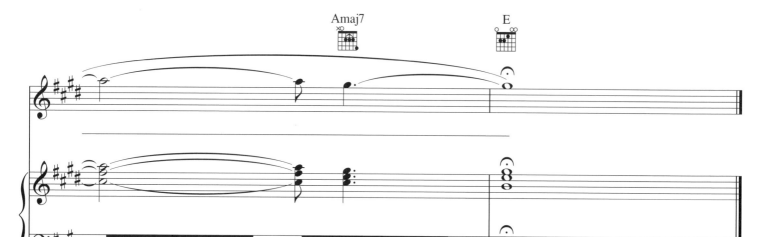

HEAVEN IS THE FACE

Words and Music by
STEVEN CURTIS CHAPMAN

Heav-en is the face of a lit-tle girl ___ with
heav-en is the sound of her breath-ing deep, ___

dark brown eyes that dis-ap-pear ___ when she smiles.
ly-ing on my chest, fall-ing fast a-sleep ___ while I sing.

And heav-en is the place where she calls my name, ___ says, ___
And heav-en is the weight of her in my arms, ___ be -

Copyright © 2009 Primary Wave Brian (Chapman Sp Acct) and One Blue Petal Music
All Rights Administered by Wixen Music Publishing, Inc.
All Rights Reserved   Used by Permission

"Dad - dy, please come __ play with me __ for a while." __
ing there to keep her __ safe from harm __ while she dreams. __

God, I know it's all of this __ and so __

__ much more, __ but God, You know that this is what __ I'm ach
long -

-ing for. __ God, You know I just can't see __ be -
-ing

yond the ___ door.   So right now,

But in my ___ mind's eye, ___ I can see ___ a place ___ where Your glo-

-ry fills ___ ev-'ry emp - ty space. ___ All the can-

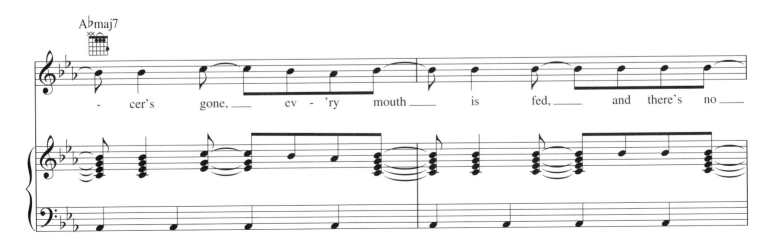

-cer's gone, ___ ev-'ry mouth ___ is fed, ___ and there's no ___

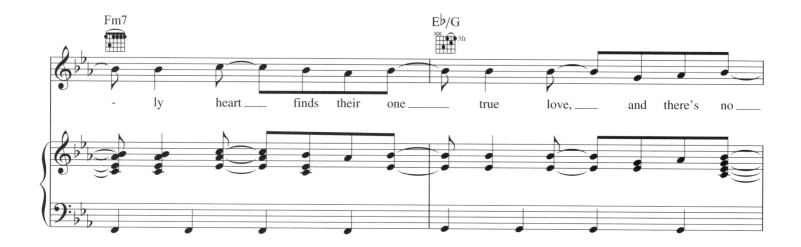

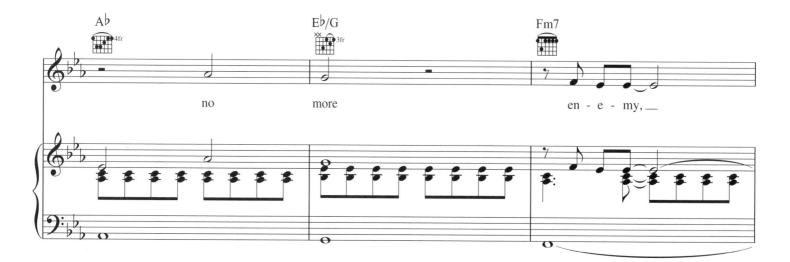

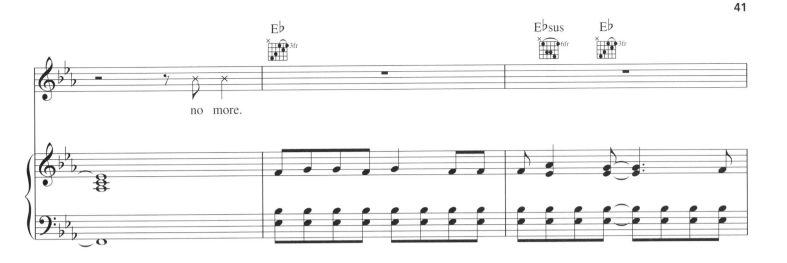

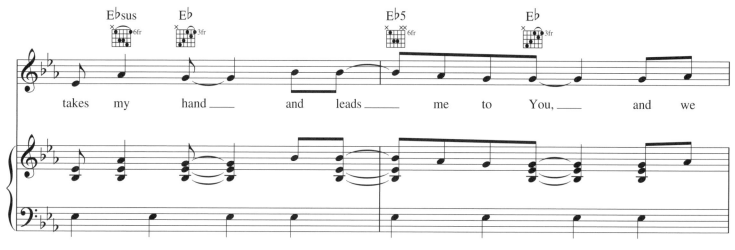

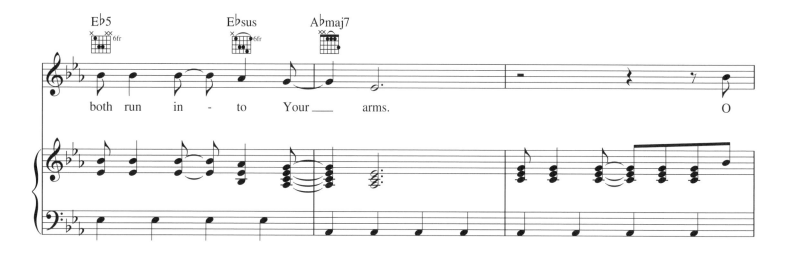

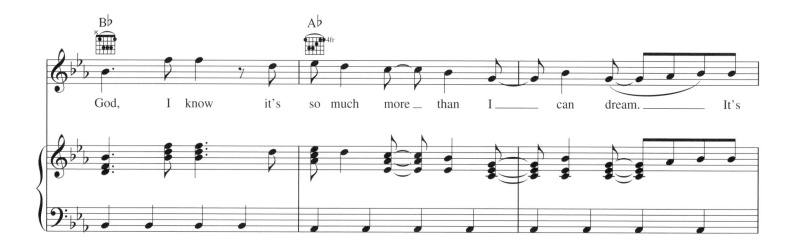

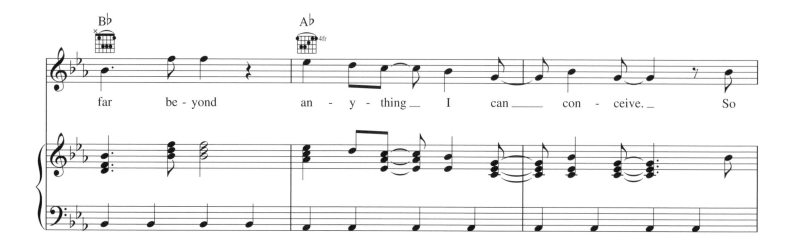

God, You know I'm trust - ing You ___ un - til I see ___

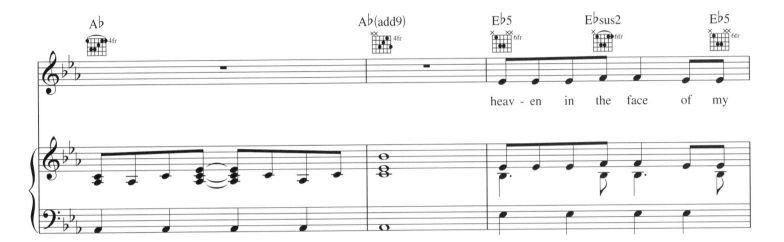

heav - en in the face of my

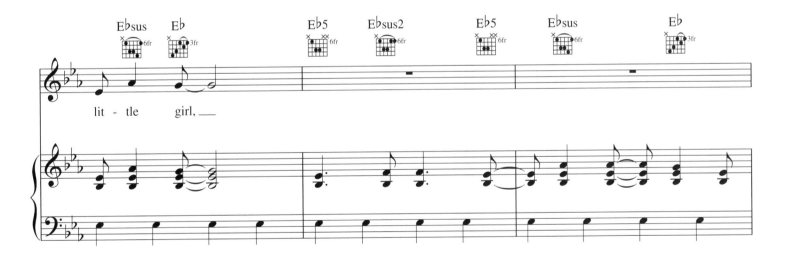

lit - tle girl, ___

heav - en in the face of my lit - tle girl. ___

rit.

GIVE ME JESUS

Words and Music by
JEREMY CAMP

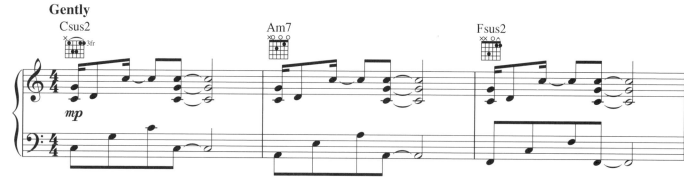

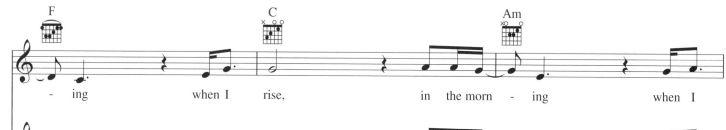

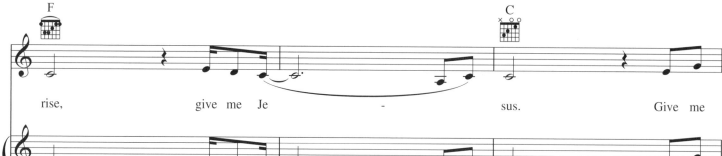

© 2006 THIRSTY MOON RIVER PUBLISHING (ASCAP) and STOLEN PRIDE MUSIC (ASCAP)
Admin. at EMICMGPUBLISHING.COM
All Rights Reserved   Used by Permission

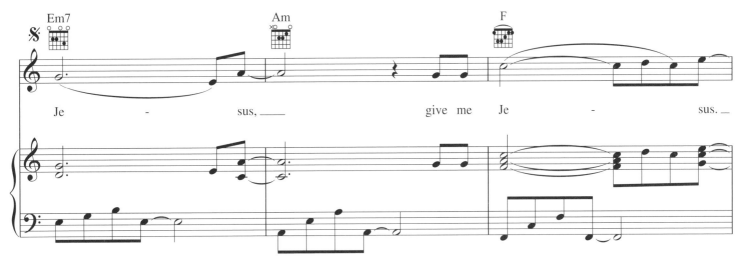

Je - sus, ____ give me Je - sus. __

__ You can have __ all this world, just give me Je -

- sus. When I am a - lone, __

when I am a - lone, __ oh, when I am a - lone, __

D.S. al Coda

give me Je - sus. Give me

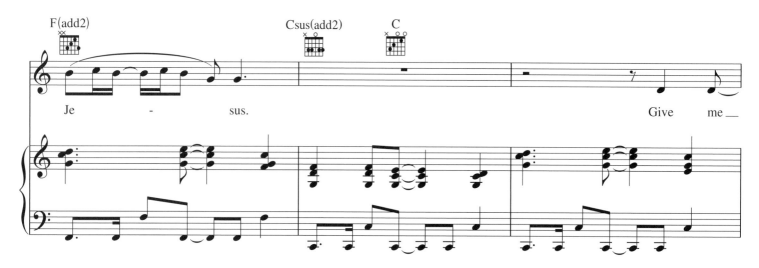

CODA

sus.

Je - sus.

Give me

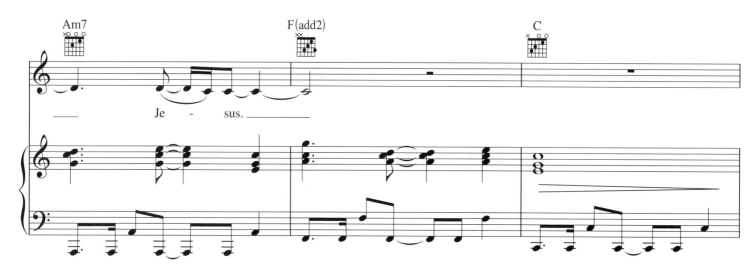

Je - sus.

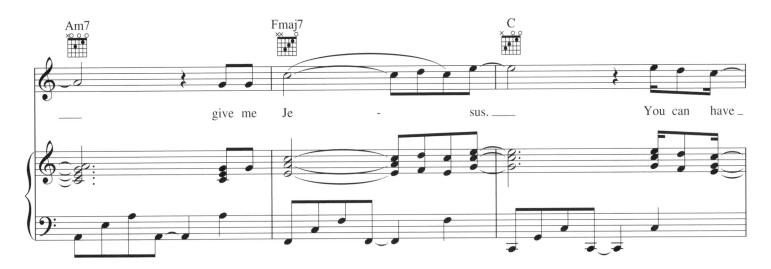

all this world, just give me Je -

sus. Give me Je - sus, _____ give me

Je - sus. _____ You can have _____ all this

world, you can have _____ all this world, _____ you can have _____

all this world,   just give me Je-

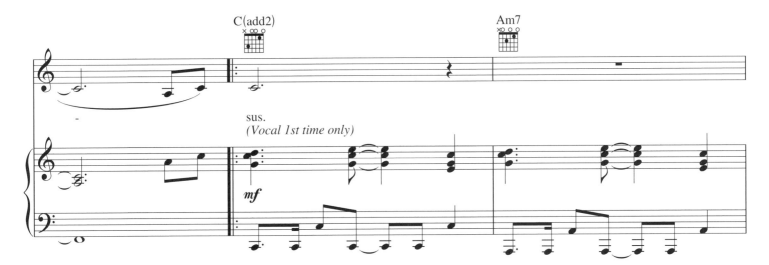

- sus.
(Vocal 1st time only)

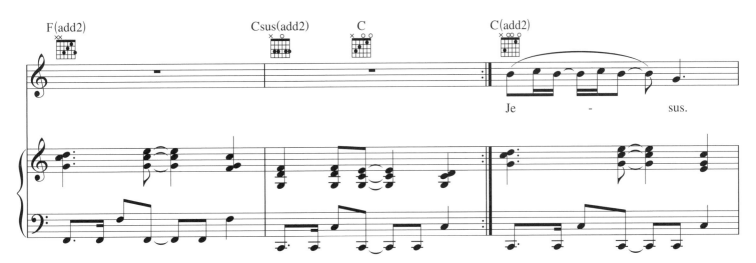

Je -   sus.

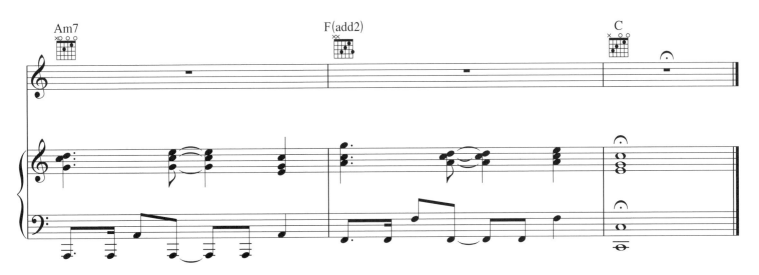

HOLD ME

Words and Music by CHRIS STEVENS,
TOBY McKEEHAN and JAMIE GRACE HARPER

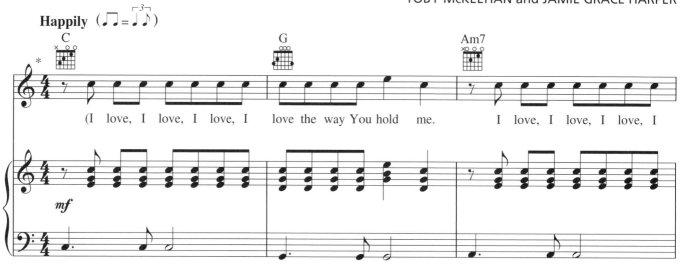

Recorded a half step lower.

© 2011 ACHTOBER SONGS (BMI), REGISFUNK MUSIC (BMI), UNIVERSAL MUSIC - BRENTWOOD BENSON TUNES (SESAC),
SONGS OF THIRD BASE (SESAC) and GRAPE JAM MUSIC (SESAC)
ACHTOBER SONGS and REGISFUNK MUSIC Admin. at EMICMGPUBLISHING.COM
SONGS OF THIRD BASE and GRAPE JAM MUSIC Admin. by UNIVERSAL MUSIC - BRENTWOOD BENSON TUNES
All Rights Reserved   Used by Permission

-lems at my job, won - d'ring what to do. __ I know I should be work-ing, but I'm

think - ing of You. __ And just when I feel this cra - zy world is gon - na bring me down,

that's when Your smile __ comes a - round. Ooh, __ I love the way You hold me. By __ my side You'll

al - ways be. You take each and ev - 'ry day, make it spe - cial in ___ some way. I love the way You

hold me. In ___ Your arms I'll al-ways be. You take each and ev - 'ry day, make it spe-cial in ___

___ some ___ way. ___ I love You more than my words in my brain ___ can ex - press. ___ I can't i -

mag - ine e - ven lov - ing You less. Lord, I love the way You hold me. Whoa, ___

oh, oh, oh, oh. ___ Oh, oh. ___ I love ___ the way You

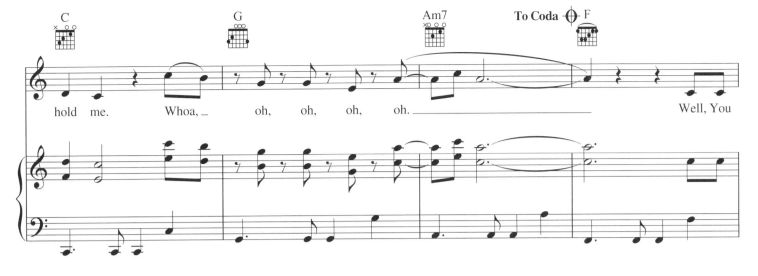

hold me. Whoa, _ oh, oh, oh, oh. _____ Well, You

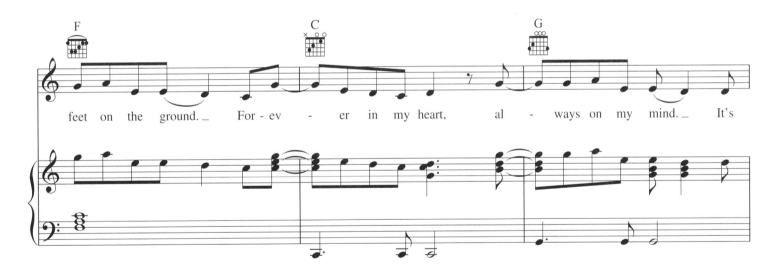

took my day and You flipped it a - round, _ calmed _ the tid - al wave and put my

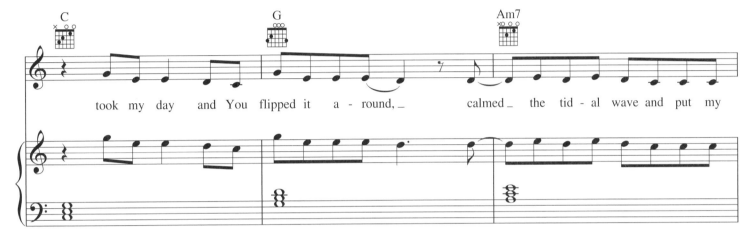

feet on the ground. _ For - ev - er in my heart, al - ways on my mind. _ It's

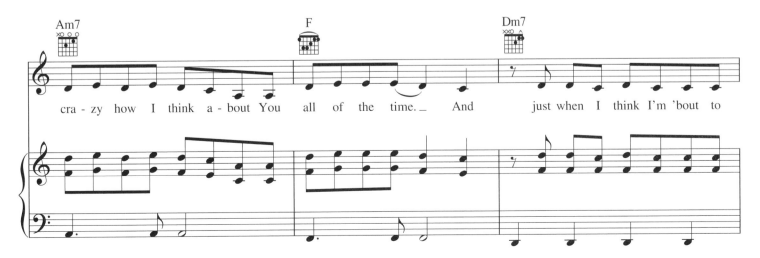

cra - zy how I think a - bout You all of the time. _ And just when I think I'm 'bout to

fig - ure You out, ___ You make me wan - na sing and shout. I love the way You

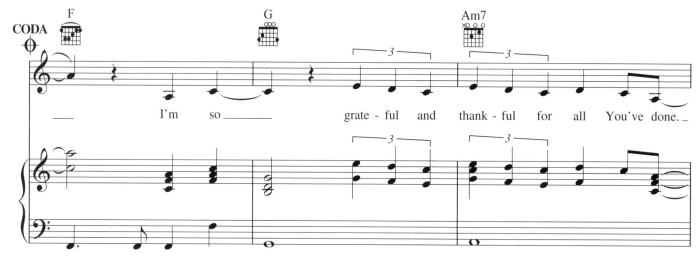

___ I'm so ___ grate - ful and thank - ful for all You've done. ___

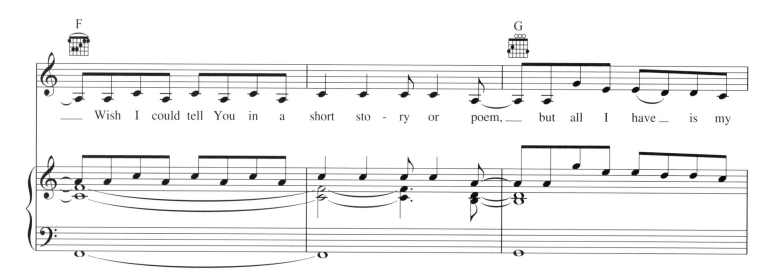

___ Wish I could tell You in a short sto - ry or poem, ___ but all I have ___ is my

voice and this ___ gui - tar. ___ And You have my heart.

Ooh, I love the way You hold me. By __ my side You'll al - ways be. You take each and ev -

- 'ry day, make it spe - cial in _____ some way. I love the way You hold me. In ___ Your arms I'll

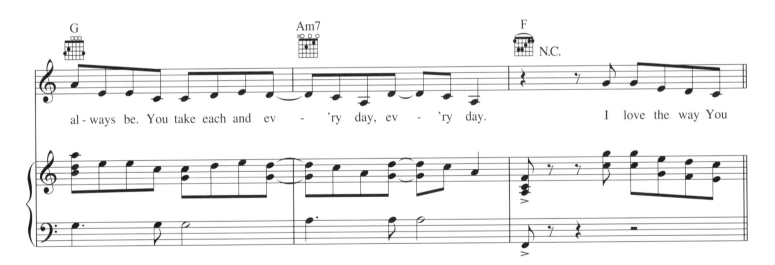

al - ways be. You take each and ev - 'ry day, ev - 'ry day. I love the way You

hold me. By __ my side You'll al - ways be. You make each and ev - 'ry day, oh, __ so spe -

cial. I love the way You hold me. In ___ Your arms I'll al-ways be. You take each and ev-

-'ry day, make it spe-cial in ___ some way. ___ I love You more than my words in my brain ___

___ can ex-press. ___ I can't i-mag-ine e-ven lov-ing You less. Lord, I love the way You

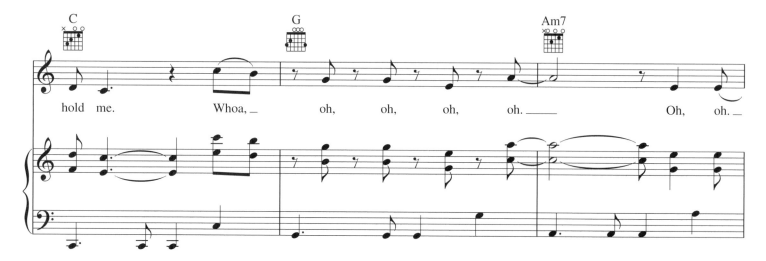

hold me. Whoa, ___ oh, oh, oh, oh. ___ Oh, oh. ___

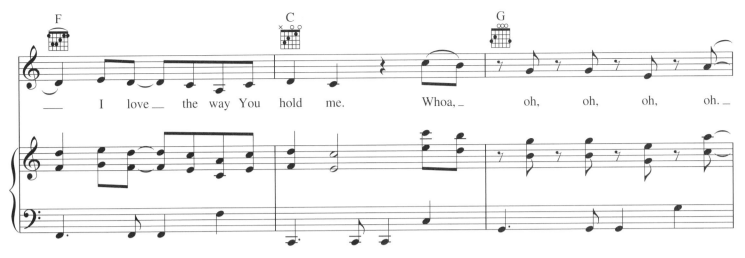

HOLD US TOGETHER

Words and Music by STEVE WILSON
and MATT MAHER

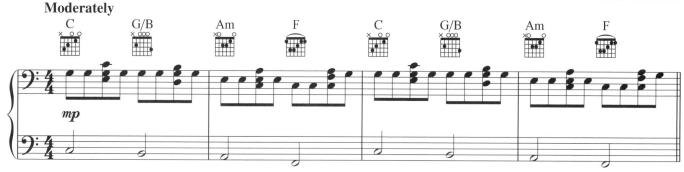

It don't have a job, ___ don't pay ___ your bills, ___

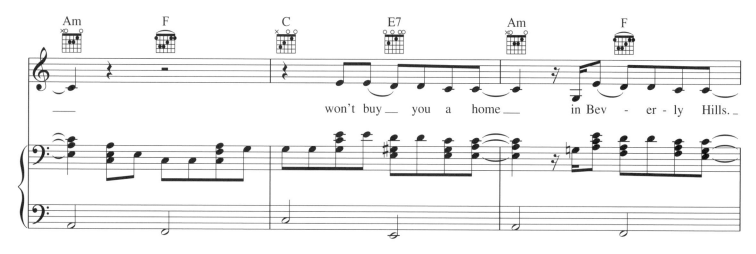

won't buy ___ you a home ___ in Bev - er - ly Hills. ___

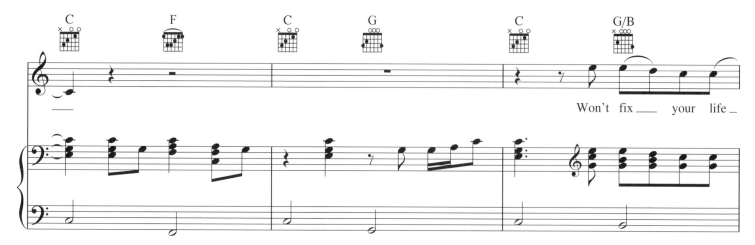

Won't fix ___ your life ___

© 2009 Meaux Mercy (BMI), SPIRITANDSONG.COM PUBLISHING (BMI), SKYLINE APARTMENTS MUSIC (BMI) and THANKYOU MUSIC (PRS)
MEAUX MERCY, SPIRITANDSONG.COM PUBLISHING and SKYLINE APARTMENTS MUSIC Admin. at EMICMGPUBLISHING.COM
THANKYOU MUSIC Admin. Worldwide at EMICMGPUBLISHING.COM except Europe which is Admin. by Kingswaysongs
All Rights Reserved   Used by Permission

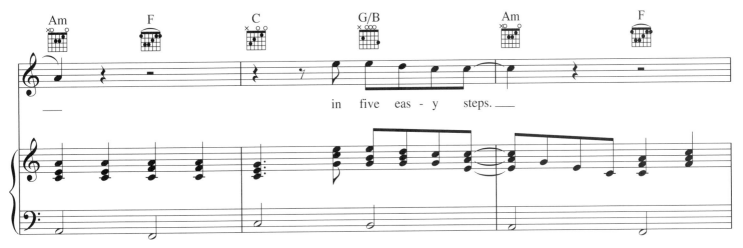

in five eas - y steps. ___

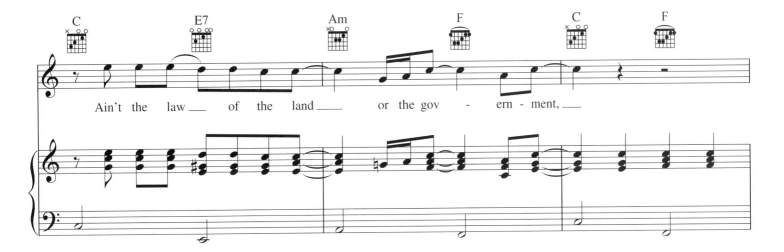

Ain't the law ___ of the land ___ or the gov - ern - ment, ___

but it's all you need. _____
on your knees. _____ And love _

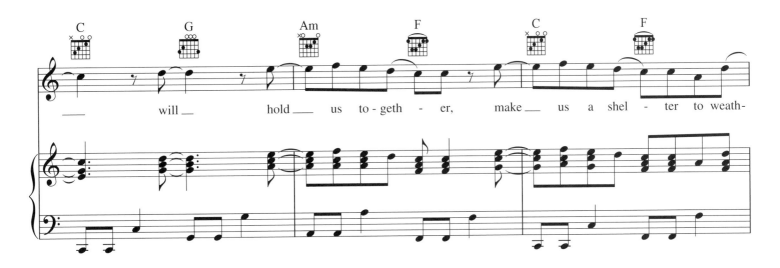

___ will ___ hold ___ us to-geth - er, make ___ us a shel - ter to weath-

-er the storm. And I'll ____ be ____ my broth - er's keep - er so the

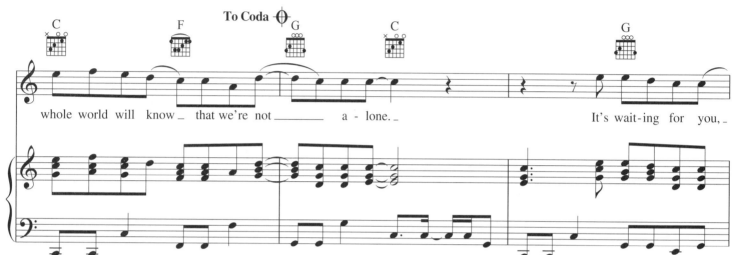

whole world will know _ that we're not _____ a - lone. ___ It's wait-ing for you, _

___ knock-ing at ___ your _ door ___

in the mo - ment of truth ___ when your heart _ hits the floor ___ and you're

CODA

a - lone. __ This is the first day __ of the

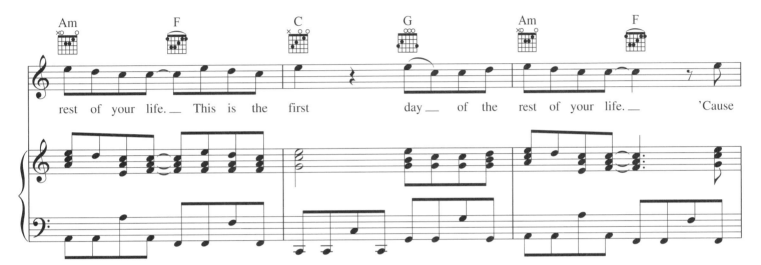

rest of your life. __ This is the first day __ of the rest of your life. __ 'Cause

e - ven in the dark, you can still see the light. __ It's gon - na be al -

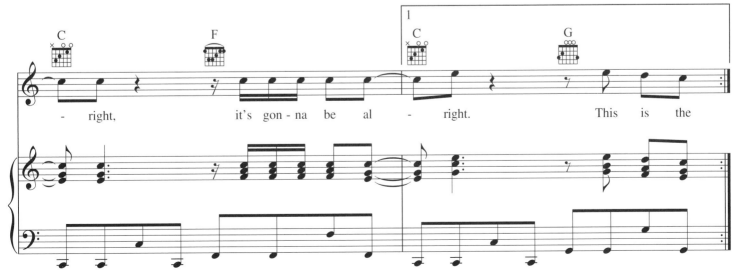

- right, it's gon - na be al - right. This is the

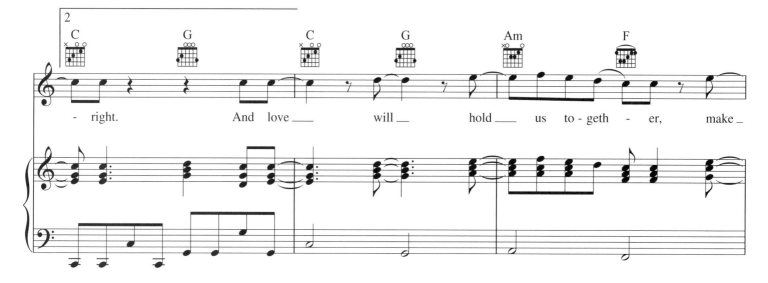

-right. And love ___ will ___ hold ___ us to - geth - er, make ___

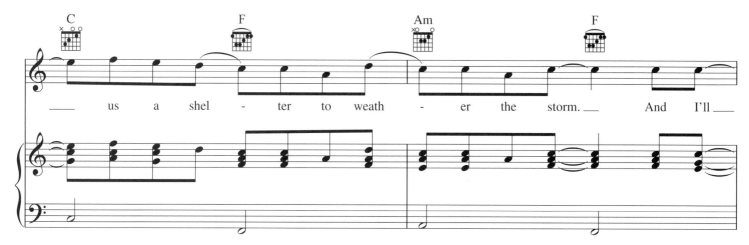

___ us a shel - ter to weath - er the storm. ___ And I'll ___

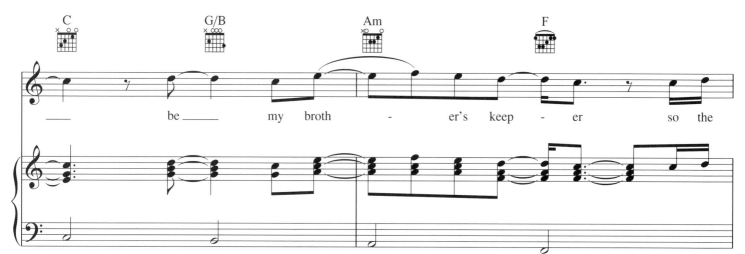

___ be ___ my broth - er's keep - er so the

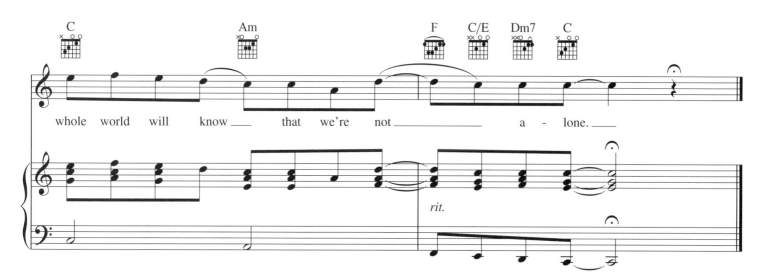

whole world will know ___ that we're not ___ a - lone. ___

rit.

ONE OF THESE DAYS

Words and Music by
JEROMY DEIBLER

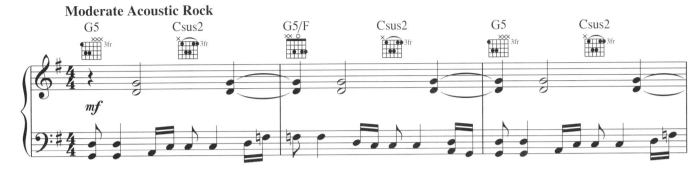

Copyright © 1998 New Spring Publishing, Inc. (a division of Brentwood-Benson Music Publishing, Inc.)
All Rights Reserved   Used by Permission

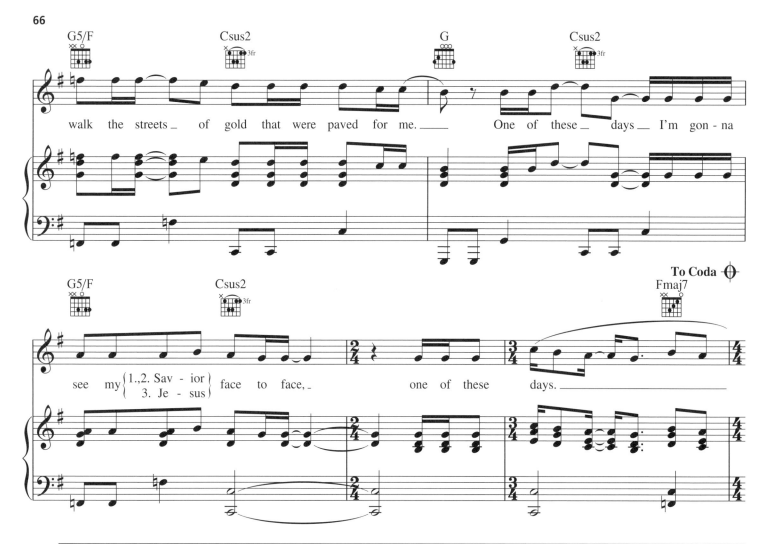

walk the streets __ of gold that were paved for me. __ One of these __ days __ I'm gon-na

see my {1.,2. Sav - ior / 3. Je - sus} face to face, __ one of these days. __

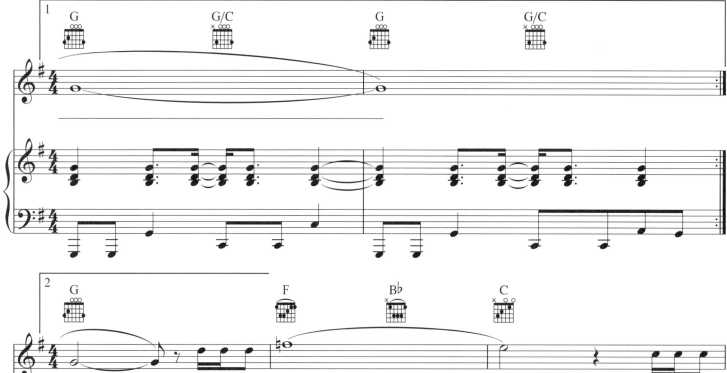

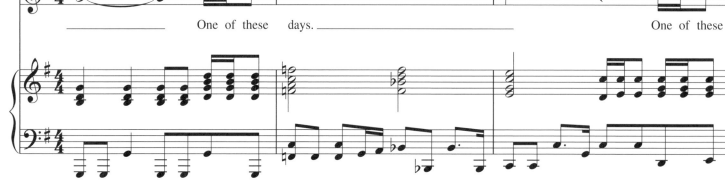

One of these days. __ One of these

I'M NOT WHO I WAS

Words and Music by
BRANDON HEATH

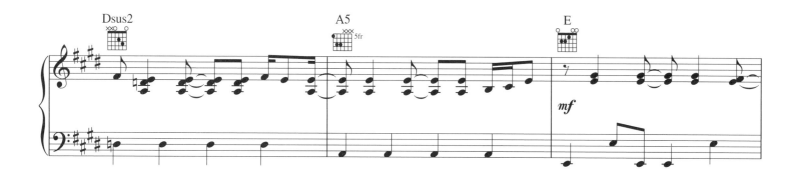

I wish you could see me now, I wish I could show you how

© 2005 New Spring (ASCAP) and Capilano Music (ASCAP)
All Rights Reserved Used by Permission

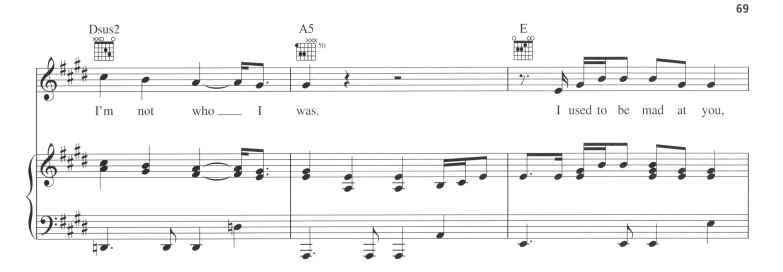

I'm not who ___ I was. I used to be mad at you,

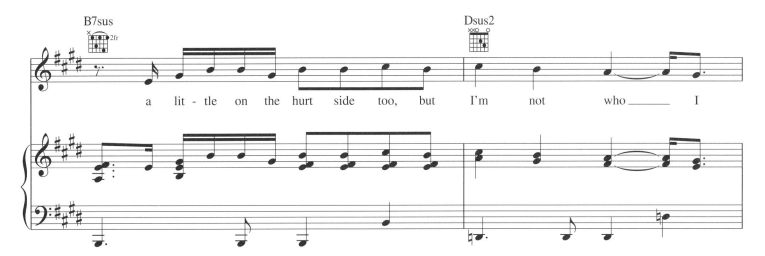

a lit-tle on the hurt side too, but I'm not who _____ I

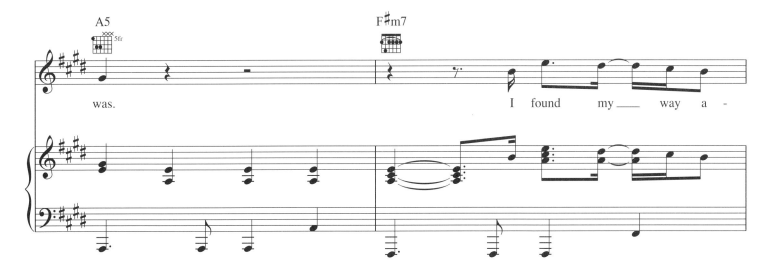

was. I found my ___ way a-

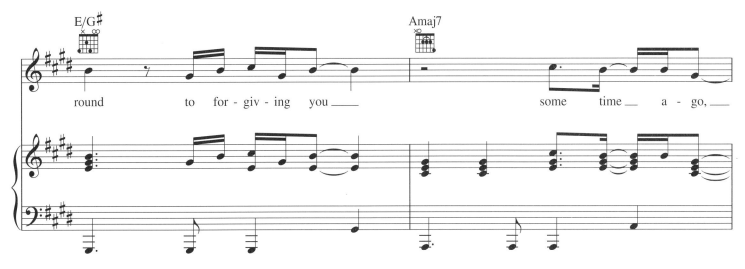

round to for-giv-ing you ___ some time ___ a - go, ___

but I nev - er got __ to tell __ you __

so.

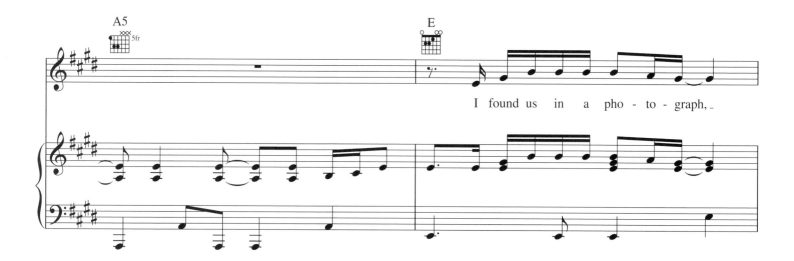

I found us in a pho - to - graph, __

I saw me and I had to laugh. You know, I'm not who ____ I

was.

You were there, you were right a - bove ___ me,

and I won - der if you ev - er loved ___ me just for who _____ I

was.

When the pain came ___ back a -

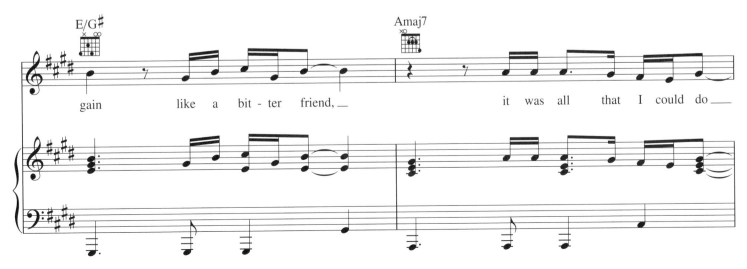

gain like a bit - ter friend, ___

it was all that I could do ___

to keep my -self ___ from blam - ing you. ___

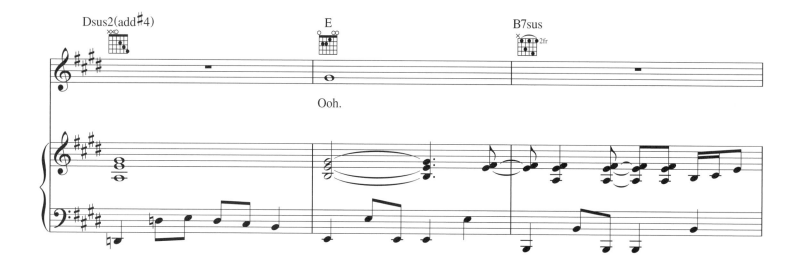

Ooh.

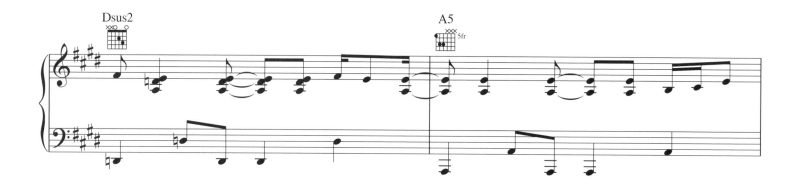

I reck-on it's a fun-ny thing, I fig-ured out I can sing. Now

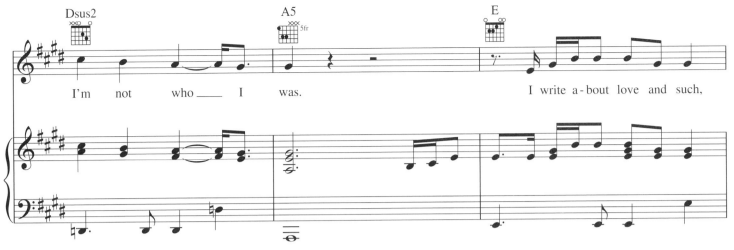

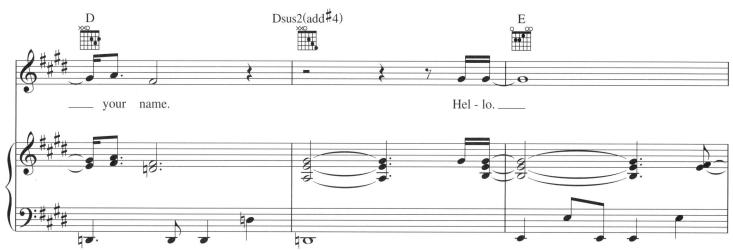

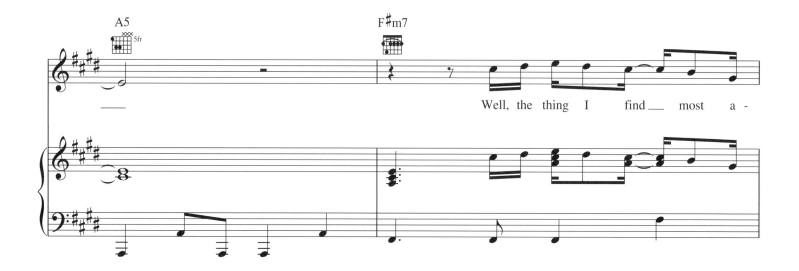

LET YOUR LIGHT SHINE

Words and Music by BETHANY DILLON
and ED CASH

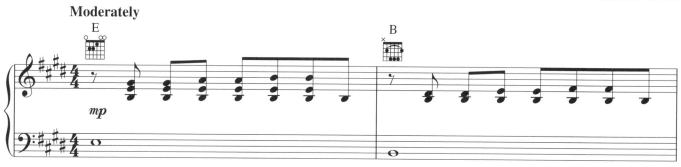

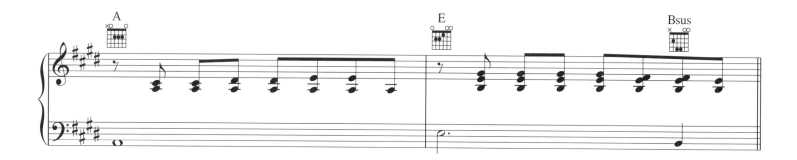

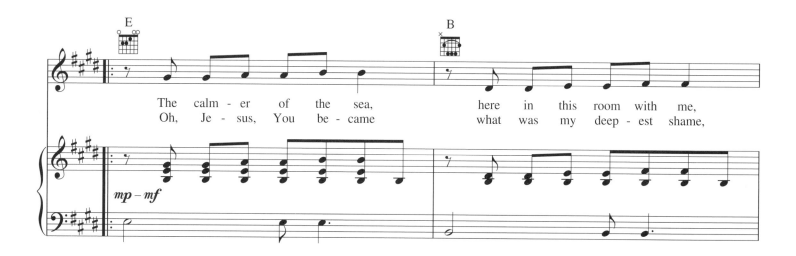

The calm-er of the sea, here in this room with me,
Oh, Je-sus, You be-came what was my deep-est shame,

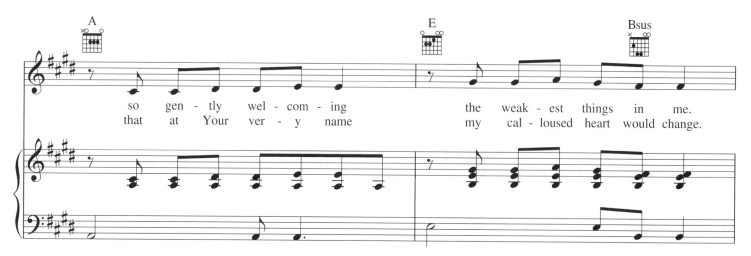

so gen-tly wel-com-ing the weak-est things in me.
that at Your ver-y name my cal-loused heart would change.

© 2007 BIRDWING MUSIC (ASCAP) and ALLETROP MUSIC (BMI)
BIRDWING MUSIC Admin. at EMICMGPUBLISHING.COM
ALLETROP MUSIC Admin. by MUSIC SERVICES
All Rights Reserved   Used by Permission

You are the blood o - ver
How could You, Per - fect One,
the door___ of my heart.
love me when I have done

What pain You spared me from,
noth - ing that's wor - thy of
how could I know it all?___
my free - dom You have won?___

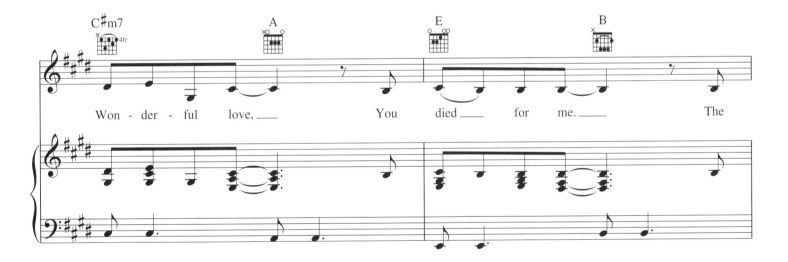

Won - der - ful love,___ You died___ for me.___ The

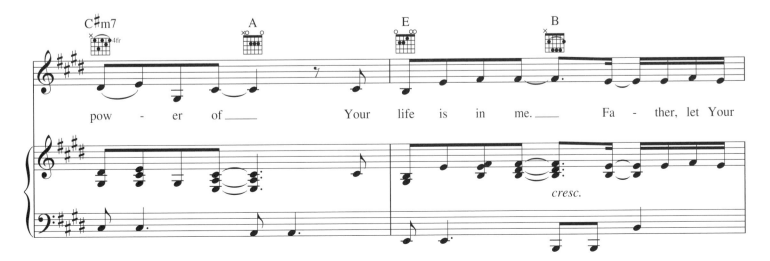

pow - er of___ Your life is in me.___ Fa - ther, let Your

cresc.

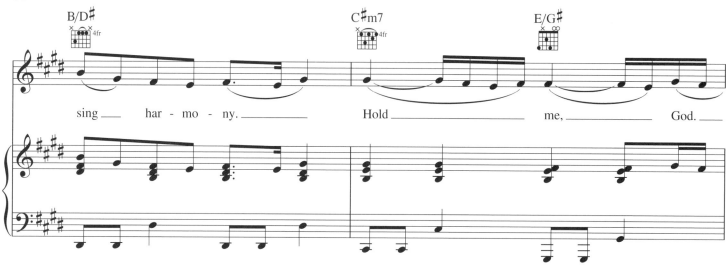

sing ___ har - mo - ny. _____ Hold _____ me, _____ God. ___

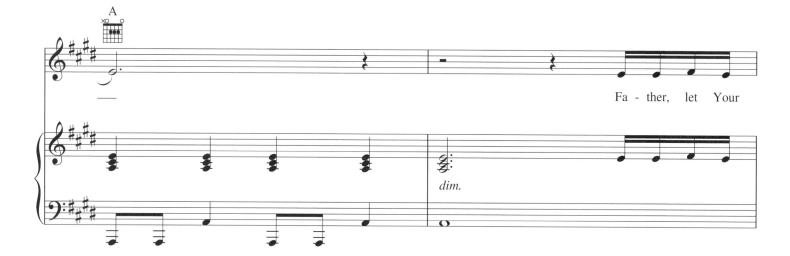

___ Fa - ther, let Your

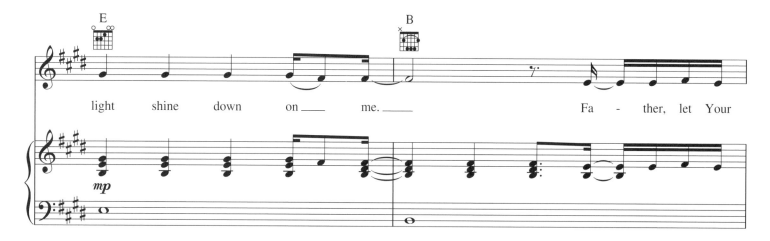

light shine down on ___ me. ___ Fa - ther, let Your

light shine down ___ on ___ me. ___ No mat - ter what the

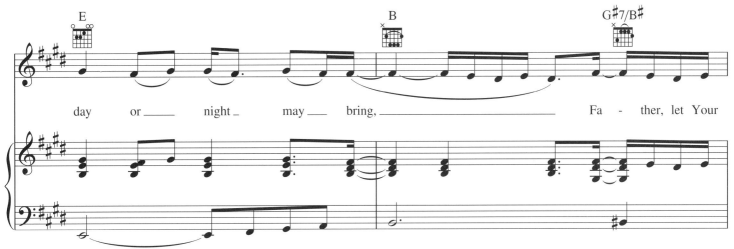

day or ____ night ___ may ___ bring, _____ Fa - ther, let Your

light ____ shine _ down, let ___ your ___ light ____ shine _ down. Fa - ther, let Your

cresc.

D.S. al Coda

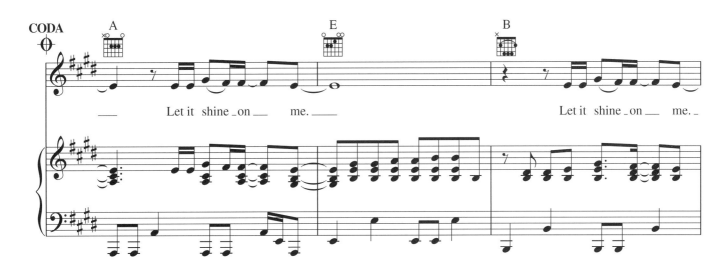

CODA

___ Let it shine _ on ___ me. ____ Let it shine _ on ___ me. _

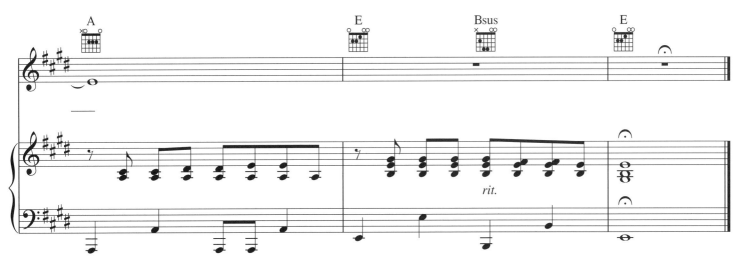

rit.

NEVER LET GO

Words and Music by DAVID CROWDER,
MIKE DODSON and MIKE HOGAN

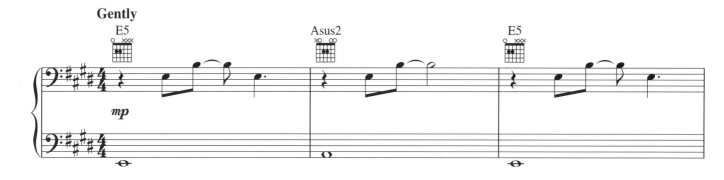

When clouds _ veil sun ____
When clouds _ brought rain ____

and dis-as-ter comes, ____ oh, ___ my soul, ____ oh, ___ my soul.
and dis-as-ter came, ____ oh, ___ my soul, ____ oh, ___ my soul.

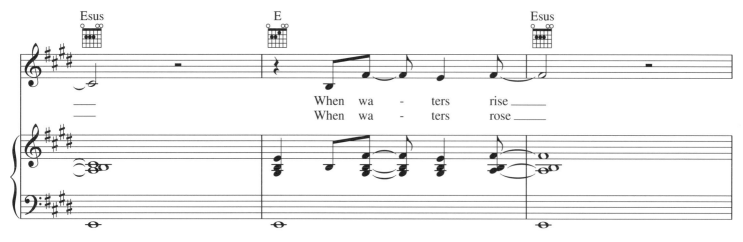

When wa-ters rise ____
When wa-ters rose ____

© 2007 WORSHIPTOGETHER.COM SONGS (ASCAP), sixsteps Music (ASCAP) and INOT MUSIC (ASCAP)
Admin. at EMICMGPUBLISHING.COM
All Rights Reserved   Used by Permission

and hope __ takes flight, __

and hope __ has flown, __ oh, __ my soul, __ oh, __ my soul, __

oh, __ my soul. __

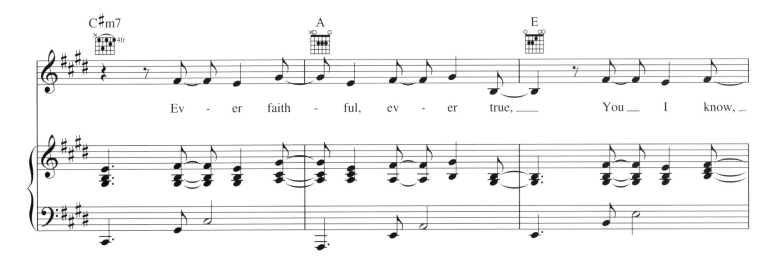

Ev - er faith - ful, ev - er true, __ You __ I know, __

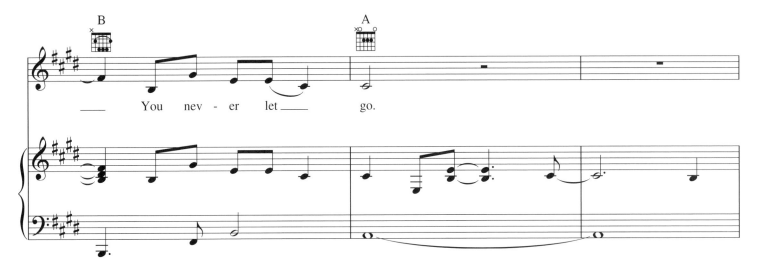

__ You nev - er let __ go.

You nev-er let___ go, You nev-er let___ go, You nev-er let___

go. ___ You nev-er let___ go, You nev-er let___

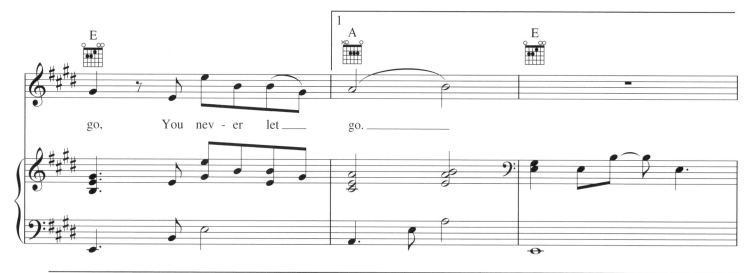

go, You nev-er let___ go. ___

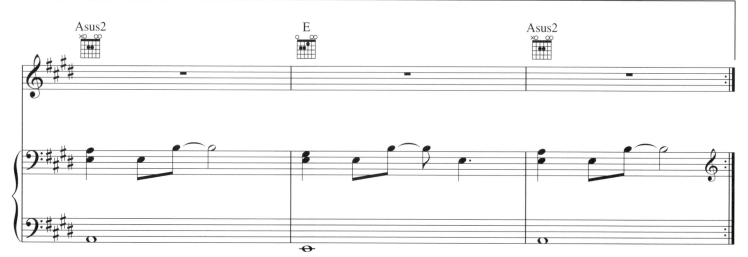

go. _____ Oh, __ my soul ___ o - ver - flows. __

__ Oh, __ what love, __ oh, __ what __ love. __ Oh, __ my soul __

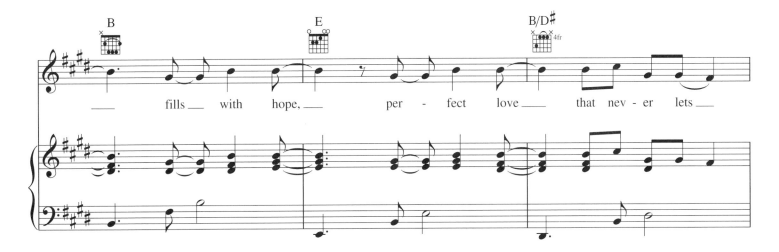

__ fills __ with hope, __ per - fect love __ that nev - er lets __

go. _____ You nev - er let __ go, You nev - er let __

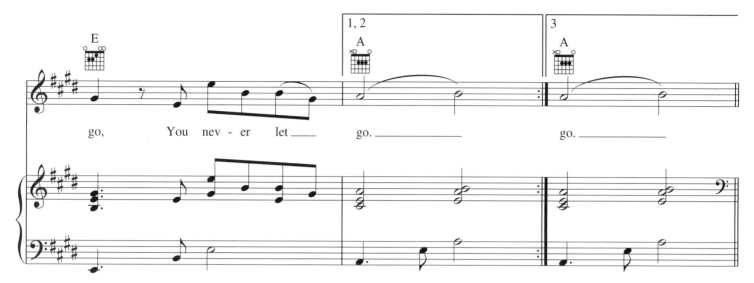

go, You nev - er let ____ go. _____ go. _____

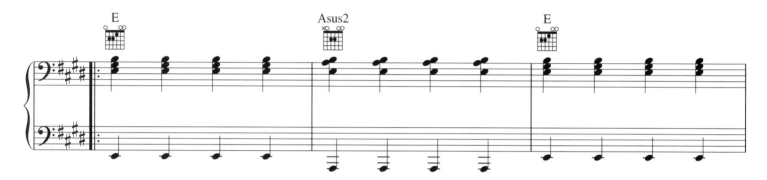

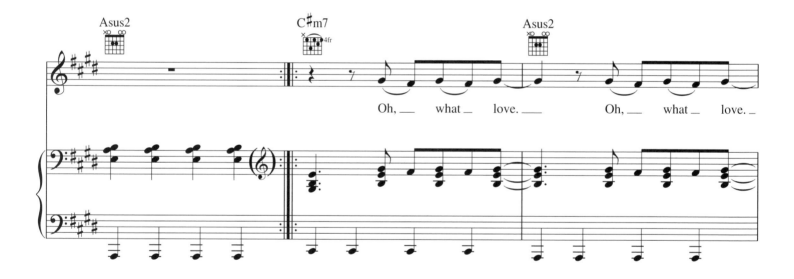

Oh, ___ what ___ love. ___ Oh, ___ what ___ love. ___

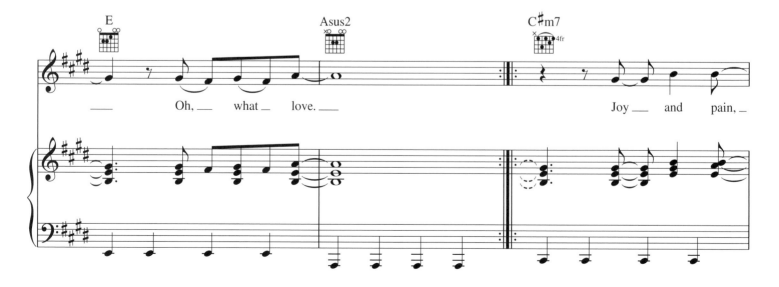

___ Oh, ___ what ___ love. ___ Joy ___ and pain, ___

in sun and rain, You're the same. Oh, You nev-er let go.

Oh, You nev-er let go, nev-er let go,

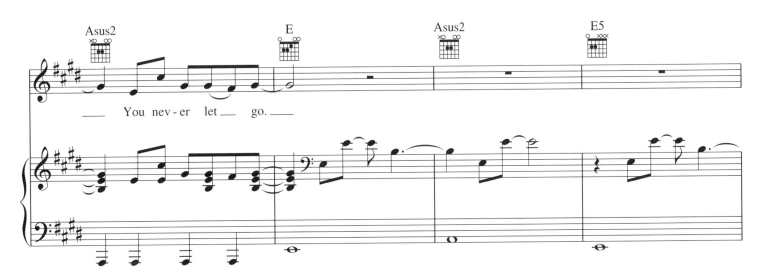

You nev-er let go.

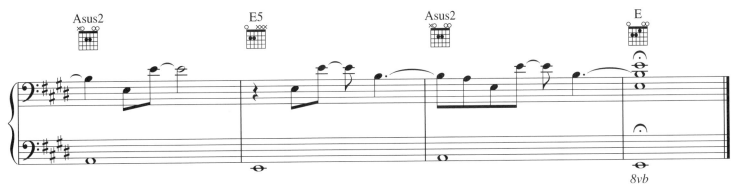

RISE

Words and Music by
SHAWN McDONALD

Folk Rock, in 2

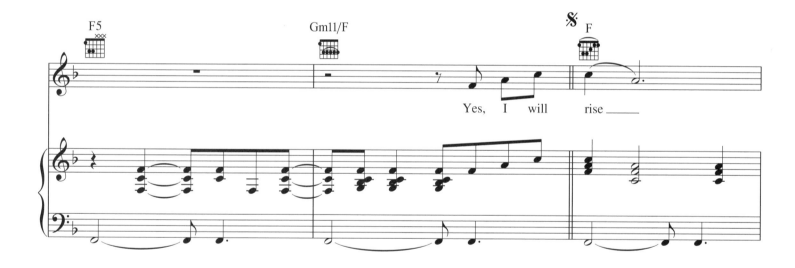

Yes, I will rise _____

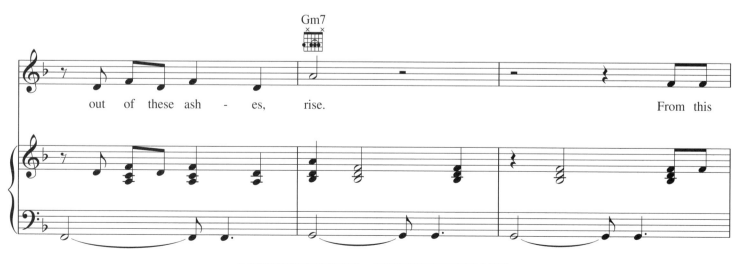

out of these ash - es, rise. From this

© 2011 BIRDWING MUSIC (ASCAP) and SHAWN MCDONALD MUSIC (ASCAP)
Admin. at EMICMGPUBLISHING.COM
All Rights Reserved   Used by Permission

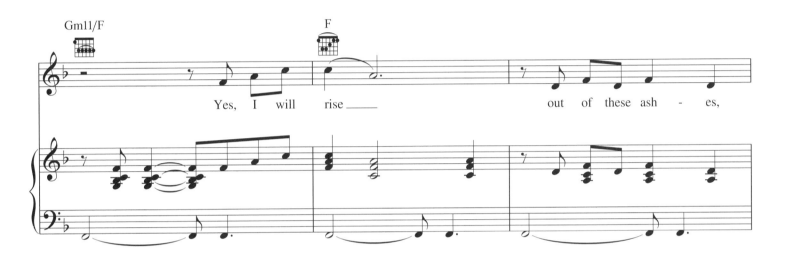

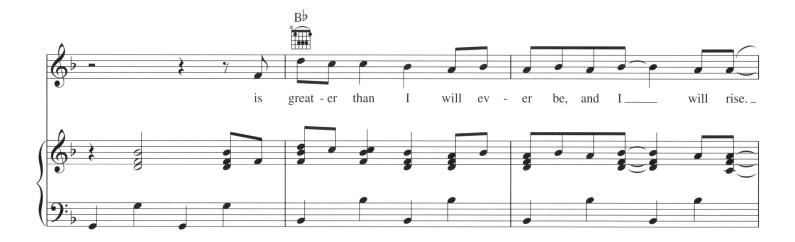

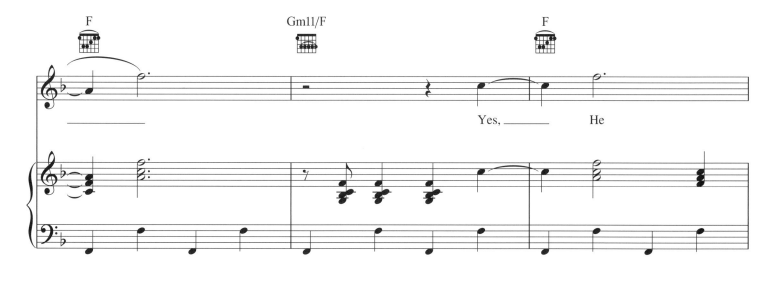

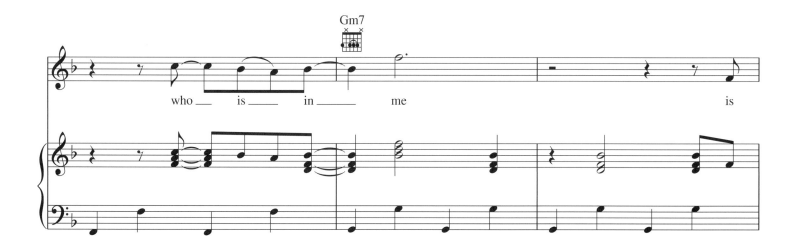

great-er than I will ev-er be, and I ____ will rise. ____

Do do do ____ do ____ do ____ do.

Do do do ____ do ____ do ____ do. Do do do ____

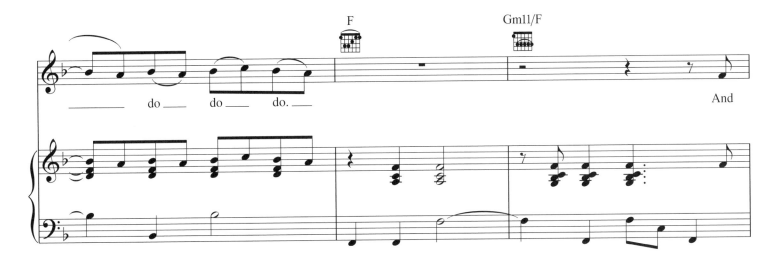

____ do ____ do ____ do. ____ And

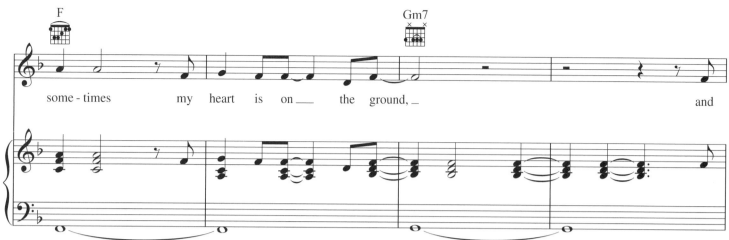

some - times my heart is on ___ the ground, ___ and

hope is no - where to ___ be found. ___

Love is a fig - ment I ___ once knew, ___

___ yet I hold on to

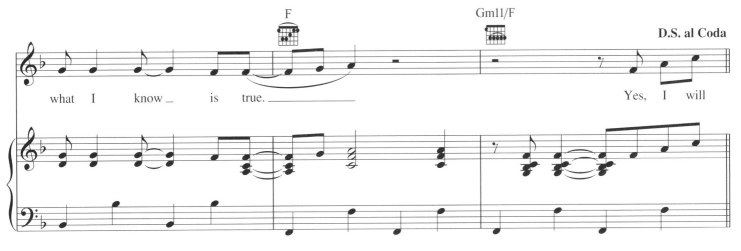

D.S. al Coda

what I know is true. Yes, I will

Well, I

keep on com - ing to this place that I

don't know quite how to face.

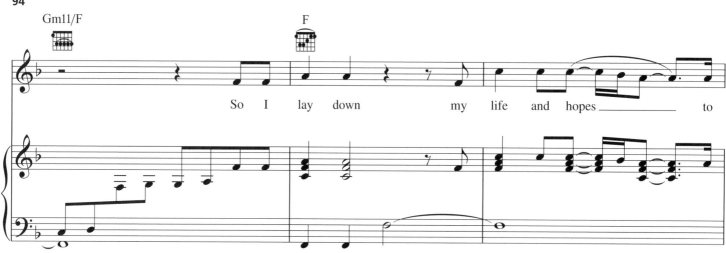

So I lay down my life and hopes _____ to

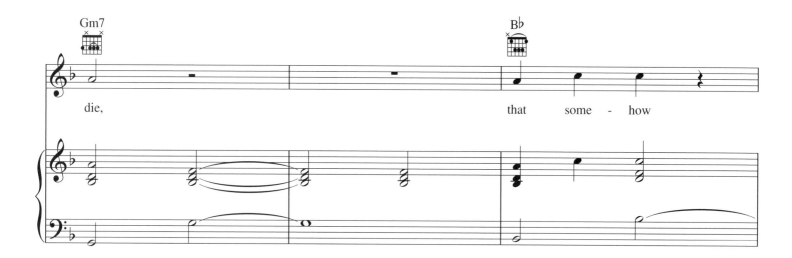

die, that some - how

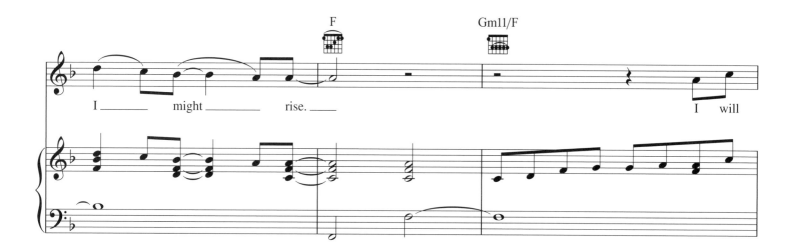

I _____ might _____ rise. _____ I will

rise _____ out of these ash - es, rise.

From this trou - ble I've found and this rub - ble on the ground, __ I will rise. __

__ Yes, I will rise __

out of these ash - es, rise. From this

trou - ble I've found and this rub - ble on the ground, __ I will rise. __

'Cause _____ He who ___ is ____ in ___

___ me is great - er than I will ev -

er be, and I ____ will rise. _____ Yes, ___

____ He who ___ is ____ in _____ me

is great-er than I will ev-er be, and I _____ will rise. _____

Ooh. _____

Ooh. _____

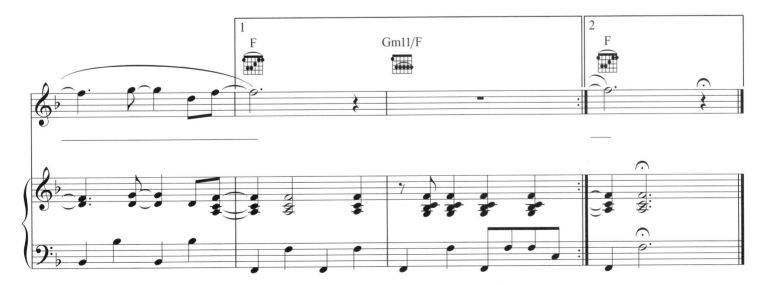

SEA OF FACES

Words and Music by JON MICAH SUMRALL,
KYLE MITCHELL, JAMES MEAD,
RYAN SHROUT and AARON SPRINKLE

Moderate Rock Ballad

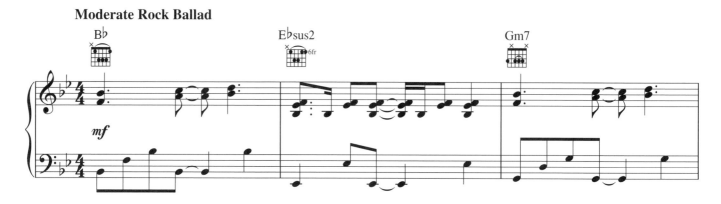

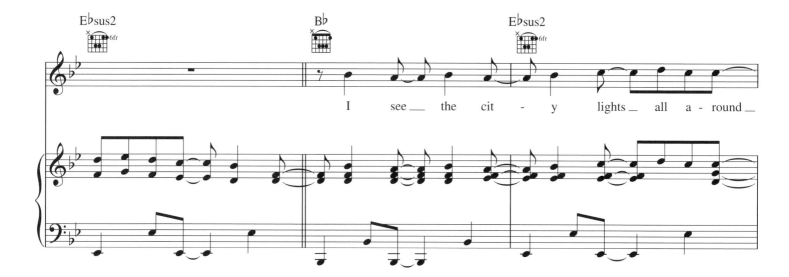

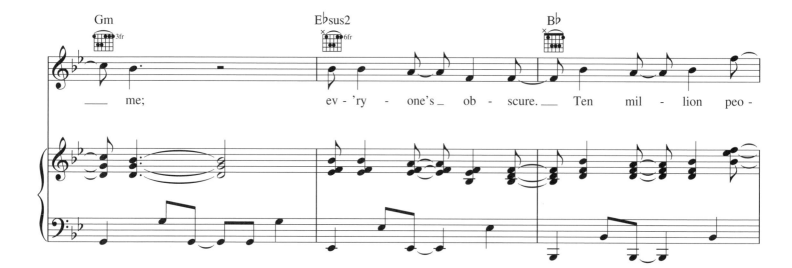

© 2004 THIRSTY MOON RIVER PUBLISHING, INC. (ASCAP), INDECISIVE MUSIC PUBLISHING (ASCAP), SPINNING AUDIO VORTEX, INC. (BMI) and SOLID PEOPLE SONGS (BMI)
Admin. at EMICMGPUBLISHING.COM
All Rights Reserved   Used by Permission

- ple, each with their prob - lems. Why should an - y - one care? And

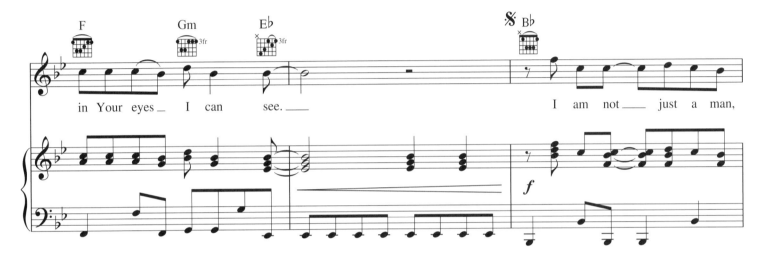

in Your eyes I can see. I am not just a man,

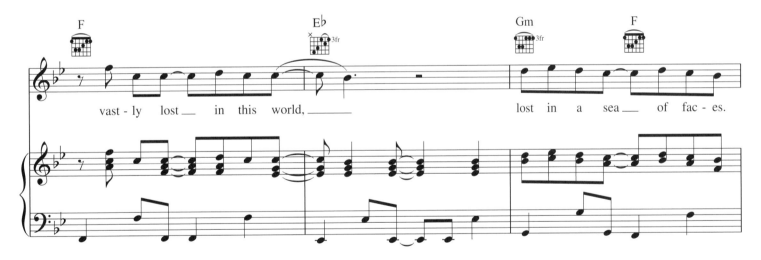

vast - ly lost in this world, lost in a sea of fac - es.

Your bod - y's the bread, Your blood is the wine, be - cause You

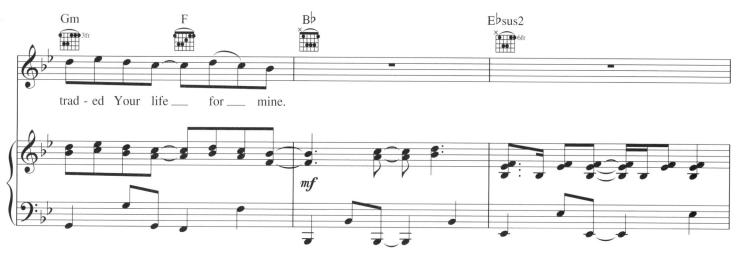

trad - ed Your life ___ for ___ mine.

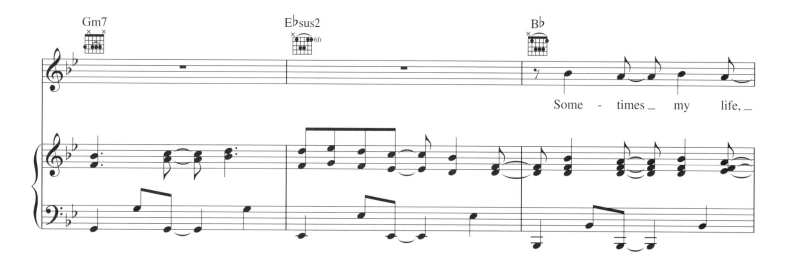

Some - times ___ my life, ___

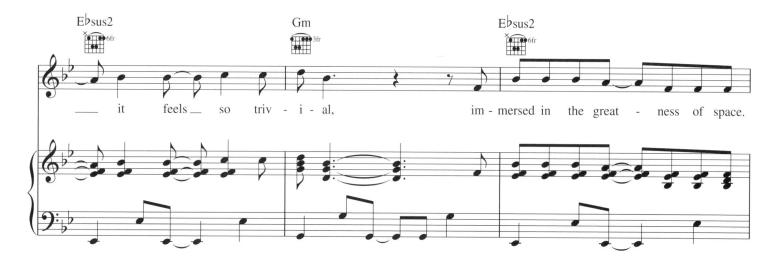

___ it feels ___ so triv - i - al, im - mersed in the great - ness of space.

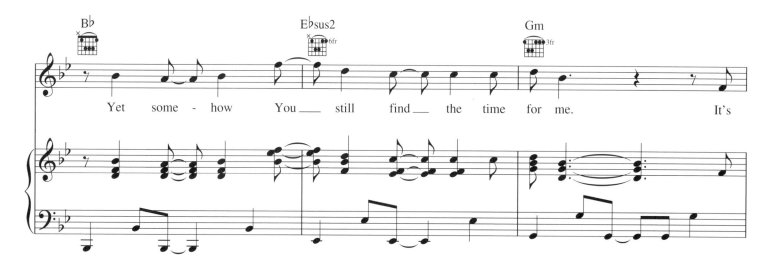

Yet some - how You ___ still find ___ the time for me. It's

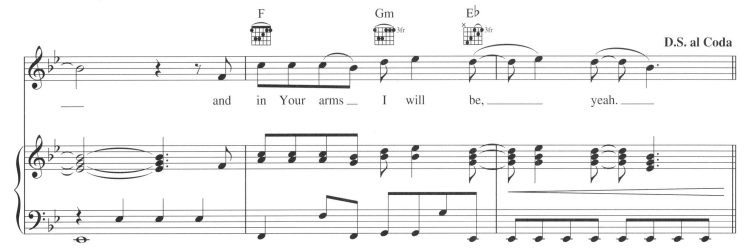

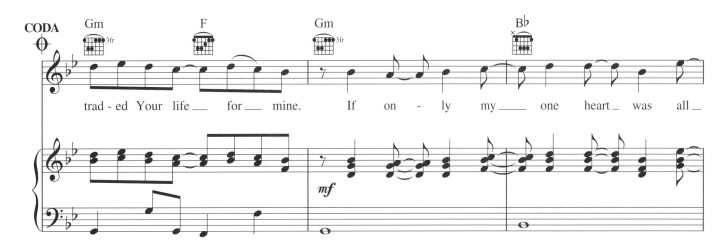

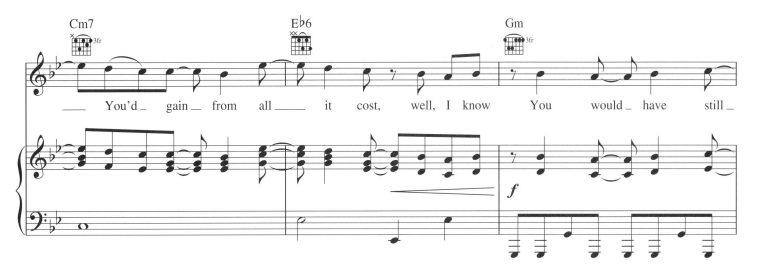

been a man with a rea - son _____ to will-ing-ly of - fer Your life.

I am not __ just a man, vast-ly lost __ in this world, _____

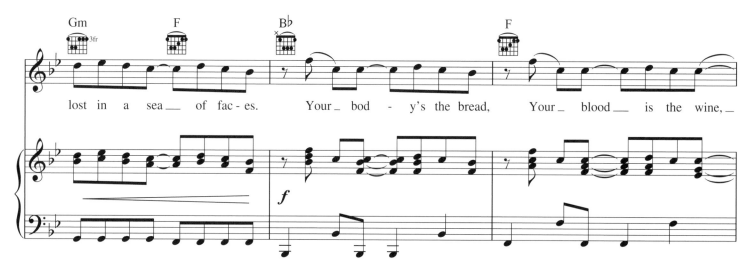

lost in a sea __ of fac-es. Your _ bod - y's the bread, Your _ blood __ is the wine, __

_____ be - cause You trad - ed Your life _____ for _____ mine.

I am not _____ just a man vast-ly lost ____ in this world, __

lost in a sea __ of fac - es. Your __ bod - y's the bread,

Your __ blood __ is the wine, _____ be - cause You trad - ed Your life __ for __ mine.

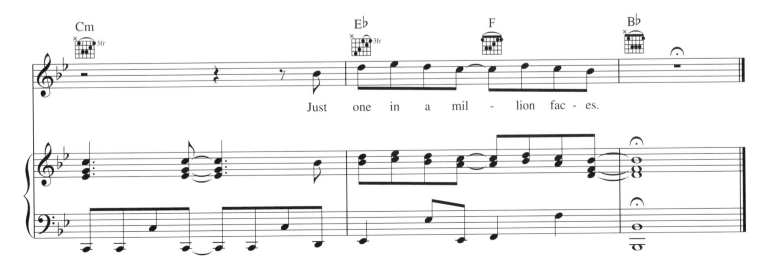

Just one in a mil - lion fac - es.

THIS IS THE STUFF

Words and Music by TONY WOOD,
FRANCESCA BATTISTELLI and IAN ESKELIN

With energy

Copyright © 2011 Sony/ATV Music Publishing LLC, Songs From Exit 71, Designer Music, Honest And Popular Songs and Word Music, LLC
All Rights on behalf of Sony/ATV Music Publishing LLC and Songs From Exit 71 Administered by Sony/ATV Music Publishing LLC, 8 Music Square West, Nashville, TN 37203
All Rights for Honest And Popular Songs Administered by Designer Music
International Copyright Secured   All Rights Reserved

please,
fines,

'cause I can't find my phone. __
while I'm run - ning be - hind. __

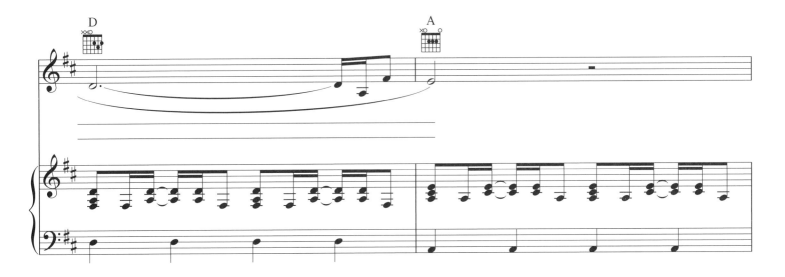

This is the stuff __ that drives me cra - zy. This is the stuff __ that's

get - ting to __ me late - ly. __ In the mid - dle of __ my lit - tle mess, __

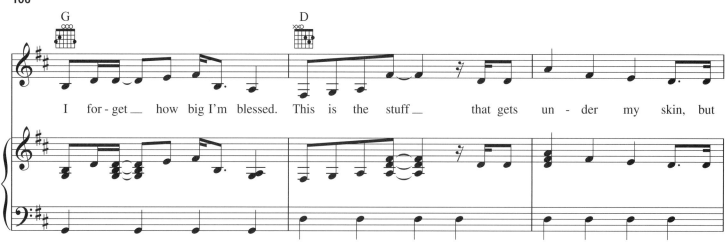

I for-get __ how big I'm blessed. This is the stuff __ that gets un-der my skin, but

I've got-ta trust __ You know ex-act-ly what __ You're do-ing.

Might not be what I __ would choose, __ but this is the stuff __ You use. __

__ For-ty -

this is the stuff ___ You use. ___ So

break me of ___ im - pa - tience, con - quer my ___ frus - tra - tions. ___ I've

got a new ___ ap - pre - ci - a - tion; it's not the end of ___ the

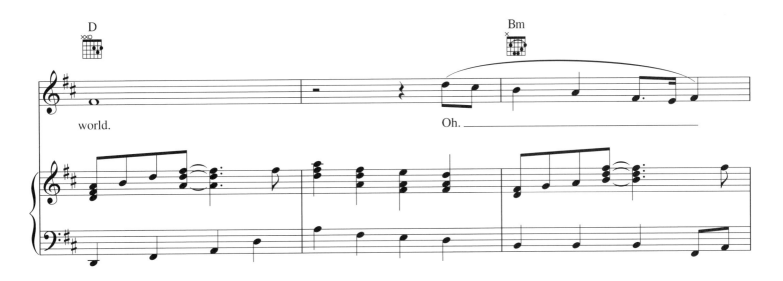

world. Oh. ___

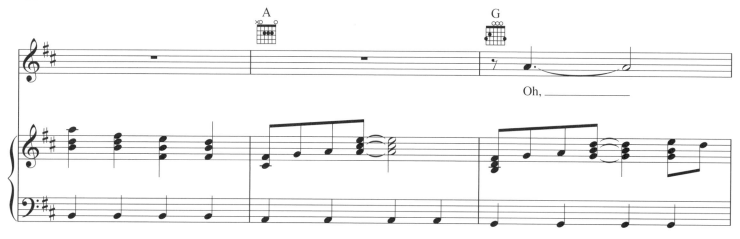

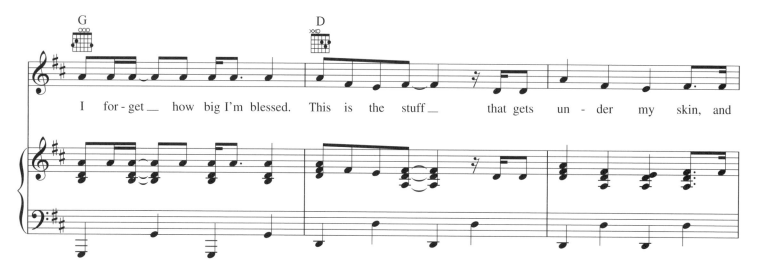

TIMES

Words and Music by
MIKE DONEHEY

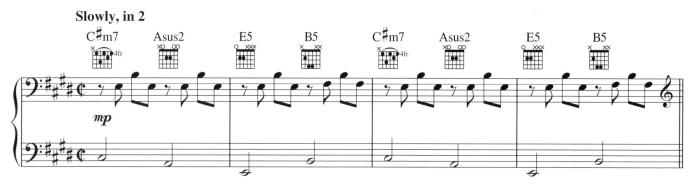

Slowly, in 2

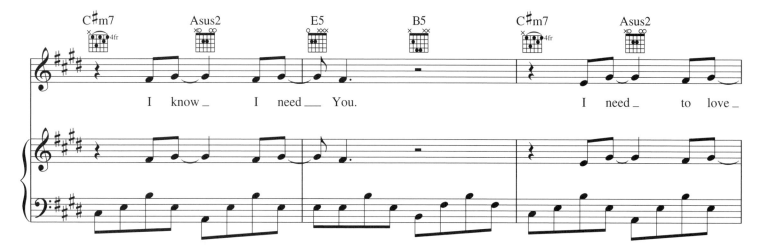

I know ___ I need ___ You.   I need ___ to love ___

___ You, _____ Lord.   I love ___ to see ___ You, but it's been so

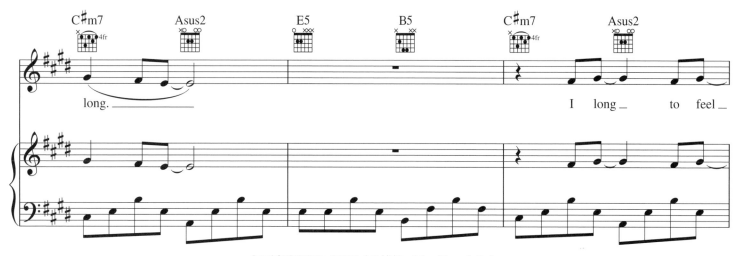

long. _____   I long ___ to feel

Copyright © 2010 Sony/ATV Music Publishing LLC and Formerly Music
All Rights Administered by Sony/ATV Music Publishing LLC, 8 Music Square West, Nashville, TN 37203
International Copyright Secured All Rights Reserved

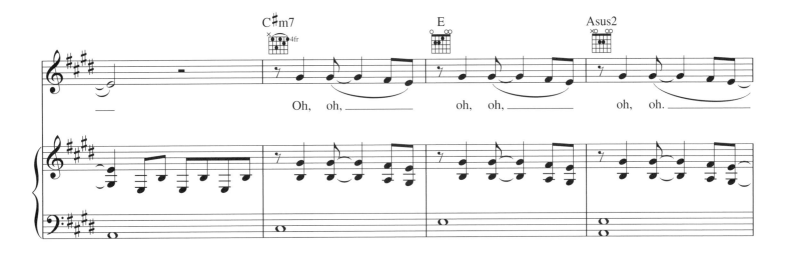

Now You pull ___ me near ___ You.

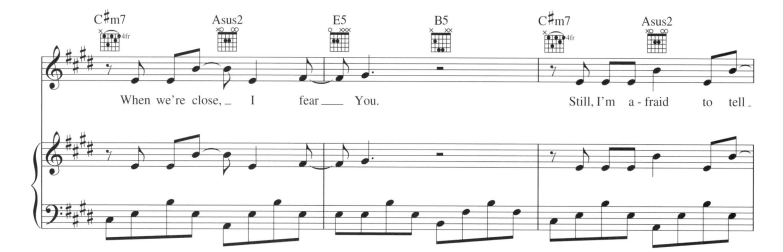

When we're close, _ I fear ___ You. Still, I'm a - fraid to tell _

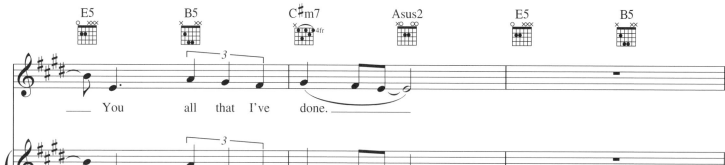

___ You all that I've done. _____

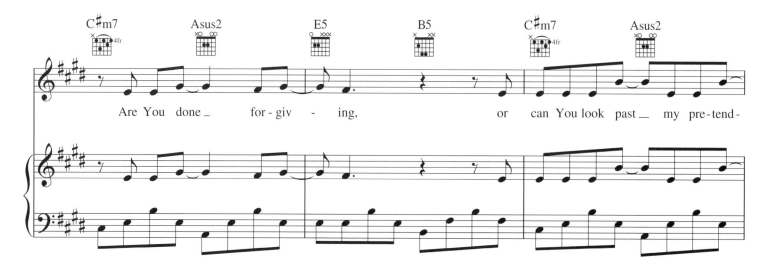

Are You done _ for - giv - ing, or can You look past _ my pre - tend -

- ing? Lord, I'm so tired _ of de - fend - ing what I've be -

come. _____ What have I be - come?

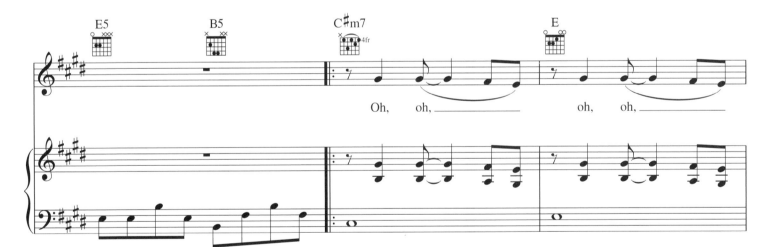

Oh, oh, _____ oh, oh,

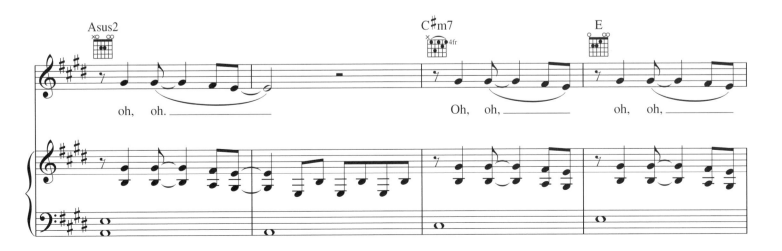

oh, oh. _____ Oh, oh, _____ oh, oh,

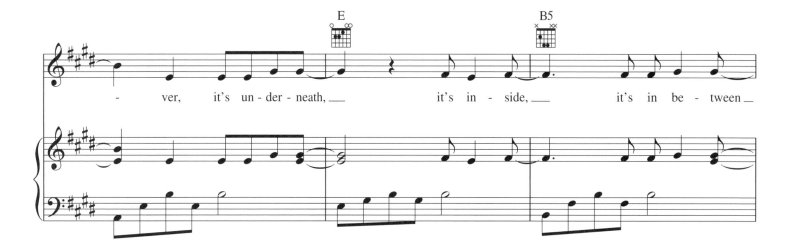

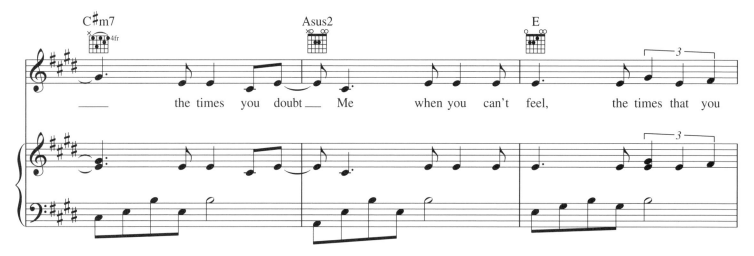

mend, the times you hate ____ Me and the times that you bend. Well, My love is o-

\- ver, it's un-der-neath, ____ it's in-side, ____ it's in be-tween ____

____ these times ____ you're heal - ing and when your heart breaks, the times that you

feel like you've fall-en from grace, the times you're hurt - ing, the times that you

heal, the times you go hun-gry and are tempt-ed to steal, in times of con-

fu-sion and cha-os and pain. I'm there in your sor-row, un-der the weight of your

shame. I'm there through your heart-ache, I'm there in the storm. My love, I will keep

you by My pow'r a-lone. I don't care where you've fall-en, or where you have

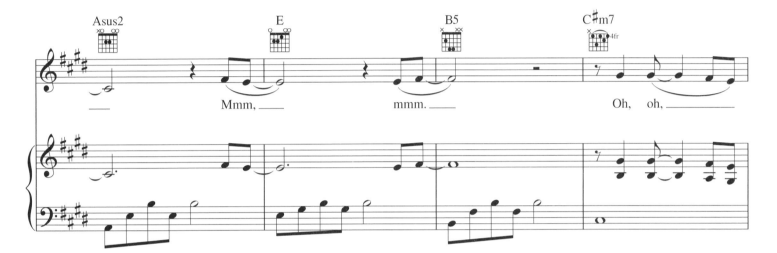

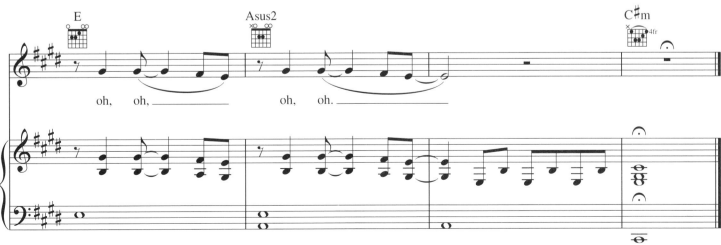

UNTITLED HYMN
(Come to Jesus)

Words and Music by
CHRIS RICE

Slowly, rubato

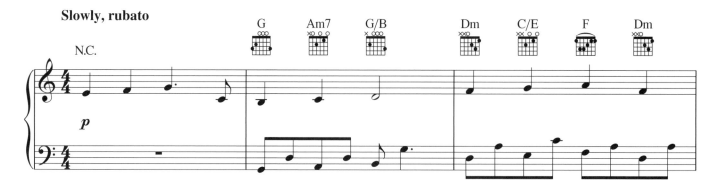

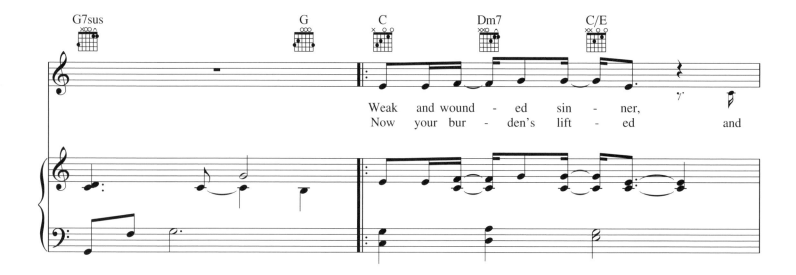

Weak and wound - ed sin - ner,
Now your bur - den's lift - ed and

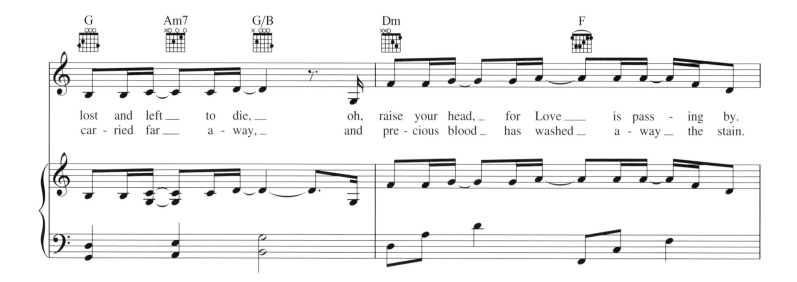

lost and left __ to die, __ oh, raise your head, __ for Love __ is pass - ing by.
car - ried far __ a - way, __ and pre - cious blood __ has washed __ a - way __ the stain.

© 2003 Clumsy Fly Music (Admin. by Word Music, LLC)
All Rights Reserved   Used by Permission

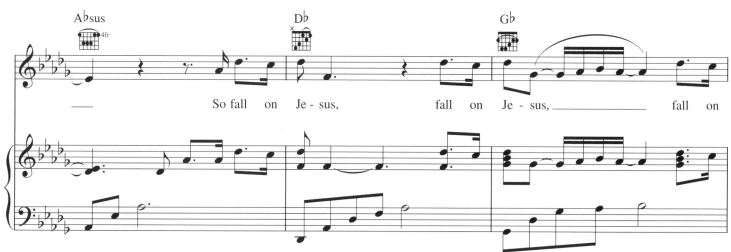

So fall on Je - sus, fall on Je - sus, _____ fall on

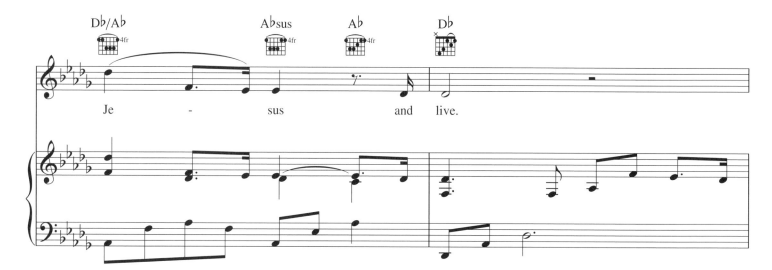

Je - sus and live.

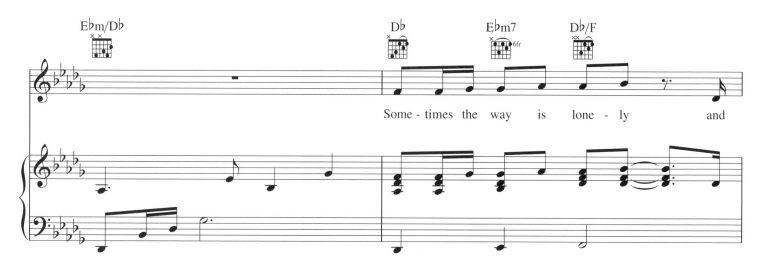

Some - times the way is lone - ly and

steep, and filled _ with pain, _ so if your sky _ is dark _ and pours the rain, _

then cry to Je - sus, cry to Je - sus, cry to Je -

sus and live. Oh, and

cresc.

when the love __ spills o - ver and mu - sic fills __ the night, and

mf

when you can't __ con - tain __ your joy __ in - side, __ then dance for

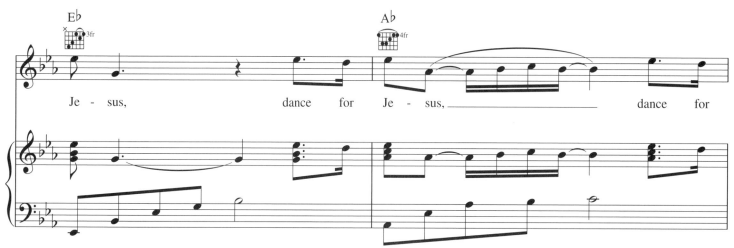

Je - sus, dance for Je - sus,_____ dance for

Je - sus_____ and live._____

___ And, with your fi - nal heart - beat,

kiss the world _ good - bye, __ then go in peace _ and laugh on Glo - ry's

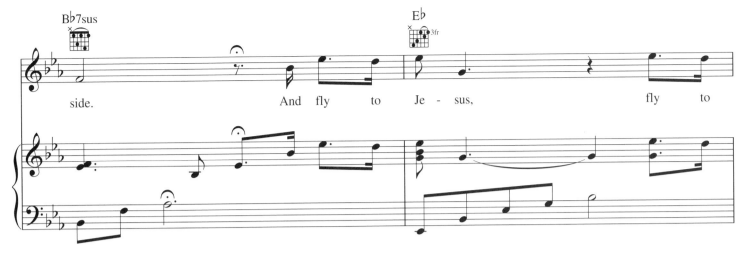

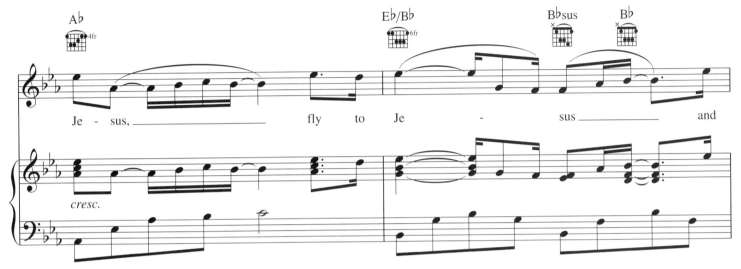

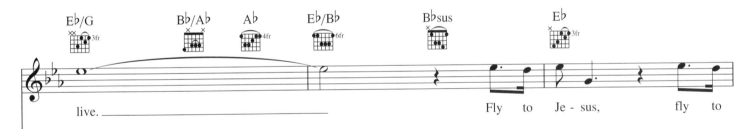

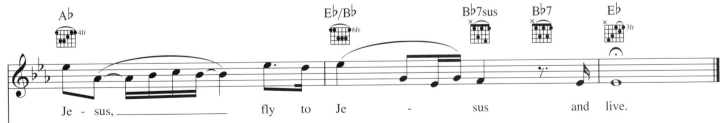

WASHED BY THE WATER

Words and Music by NATHANIEL RINEHART
and WILLIAM RINEHART

Relaxed Gospel feel

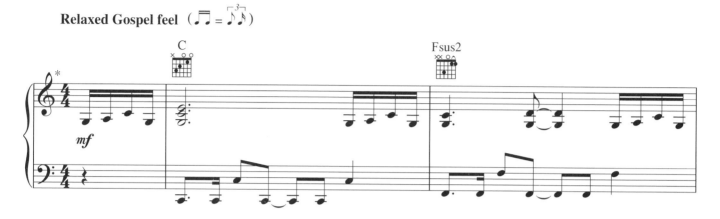

Dad-dy was a preach-er, she was ___ his wife, ___

* Recorded a half step lower.

© 2007 NEEDTOBREATHE MUSIC and WALTER EGO MUSIC
All Rights Reserved   Used by Permission

just tryin' to make the world a lit-tle bet-ter; you know, shine a light.

Peo-ple start-ed talk-ing, just to hear their own __ voice.

Those peo-ple tried to 'cuse my fa-ther, say he made the wrong __ choice. __

Though it might be pain-ful, you know that time will al-ways __ tell.

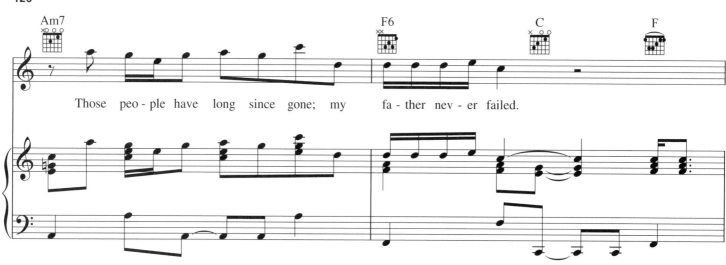

Those peo-ple have long since gone; my fa-ther nev-er failed.

E-ven when the rain falls, _____ e-ven when the flood starts ris-ing,

e-ven when the storm comes, _____ I am washed by the wa-ter.

E-ven when the rain falls, _____ e-ven when the flood starts ris-ing,

e - ven when the storm comes, _____ I am washed by the wa - ter.

E - ven when the earth crum - bles un - der my feet,

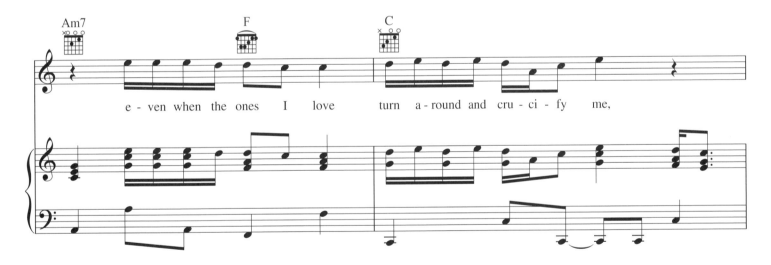

e - ven when the ones I love turn a - round and cru - ci - fy me,

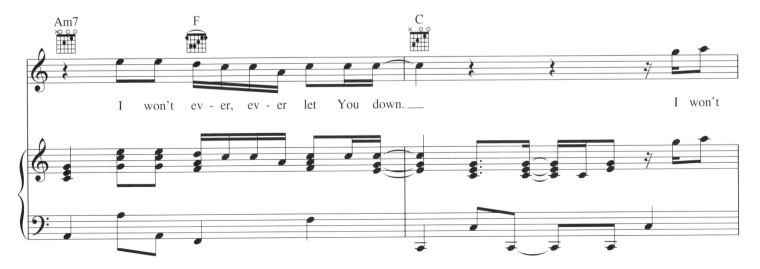

I won't ev - er, ev - er let You down. ___ I won't

fall, _____ I won't fall, _____ I won't fall as long as You're _ a - round _ me.

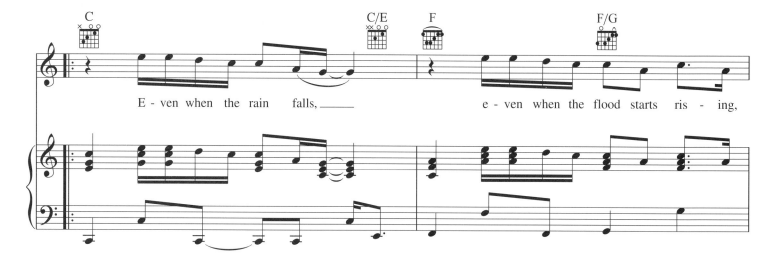

E - ven when the rain falls, _____ e - ven when the flood starts ris - ing,

e - ven when the storm comes, _____ I am washed by the wa - ter.

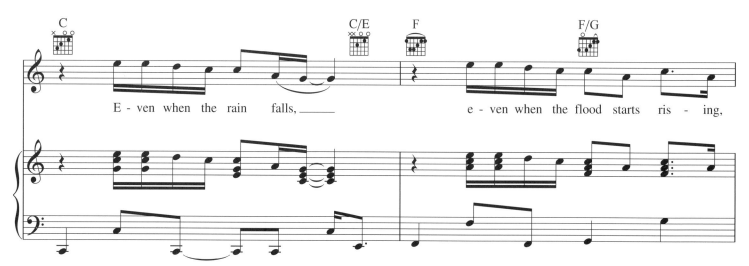

E - ven when the rain falls, _____ e - ven when the flood starts ris - ing,

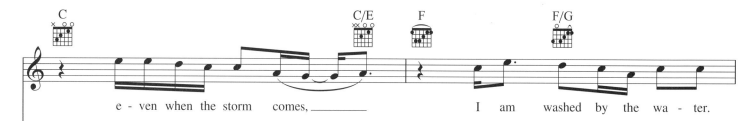

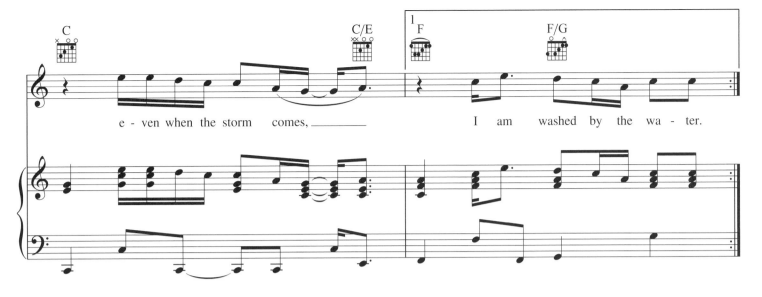

e - ven when the storm comes, _____ I am washed by the wa - ter.

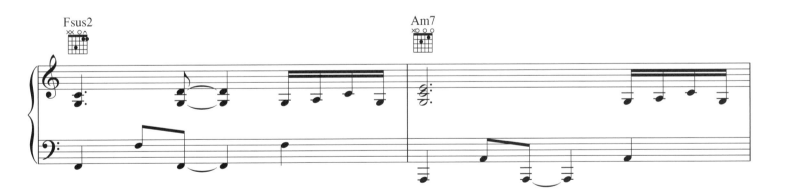

I am washed by the wa - ter.

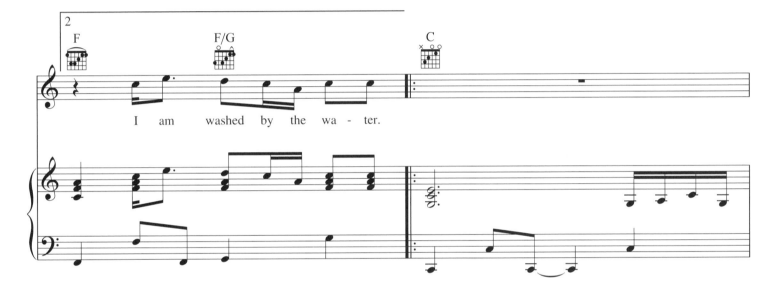

WORD OF GOD SPEAK

Words and Music by BART MILLARD
and PETE KIPLEY

© 2002 Simpleville Music (ASCAP), Wordspring Music, LLC (SESAC) and Songs From The Indigo Room (SESAC)
All Rights for Songs From The Indigo Room Administered by Wordspring Music, LLC
All Rights Reserved   Used by Permission

and rest ___ in Your ho - li - ness. ___ Word of God, ___ speak. ___

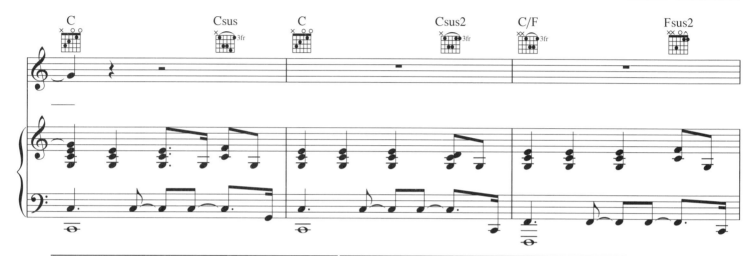

I'm find - ing ___ - li - ness. ___ Word of God, ___ speak. ___

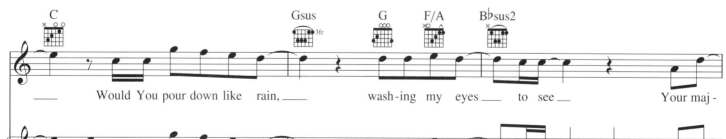

Would You pour down like rain, ___ wash-ing my eyes ___ to see ___ Your maj-

- es - ty. ___ To be still and know ___ that You're in this place. ___

___ Please let me stay ___ and rest ___ in Your ho - li - ness. _

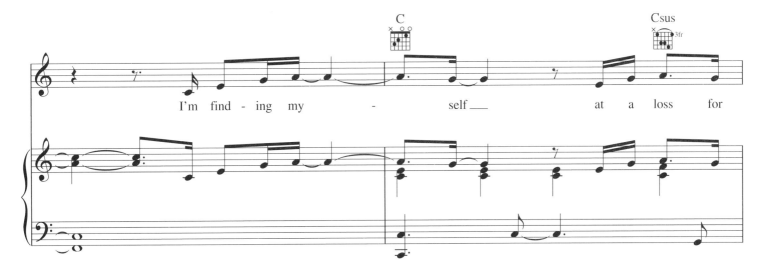

I'm find - ing my - self ___ at a loss for

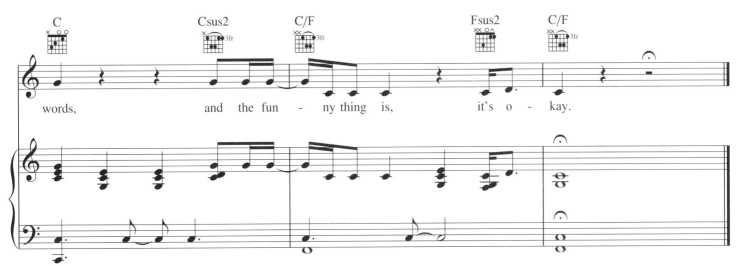

words, ___ and the fun - ny thing is, it's o - kay.

THE 21st TIME

Words and Music by TRENT MONK
and ED CASH

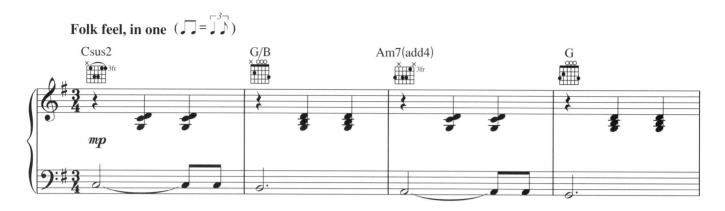

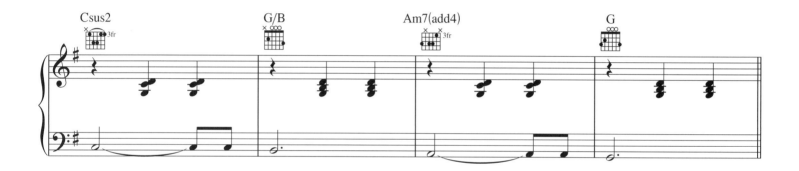

No-where to live, _____ no-where to fall. _____ He
sleeps un-der stars; _____ that's all he can af-ford. His

© 2007 ALLEN VAUGHN AND RAY PUBLISHING (ASCAP), WHOLELOTARACKET MUSIC (ASCAP) (Admin. at EMICMGPUBLISHING.COM)
and ALLETROP MUSIC (BMI) (Admin. by MUSIC SERVICES)
All Rights Reserved   Used by Permission

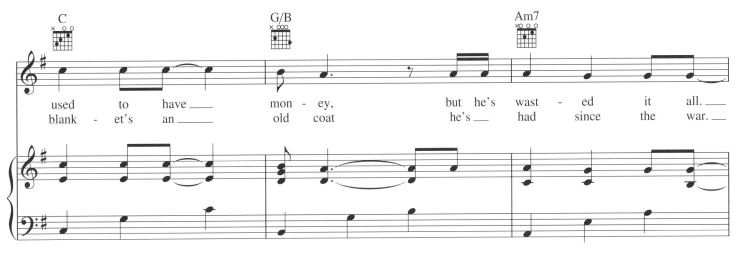

used to have _____ mon - ey, but he's wast - ed it all. _____
blank - et's an _____ old coat he's _____ had ed since the war. _____

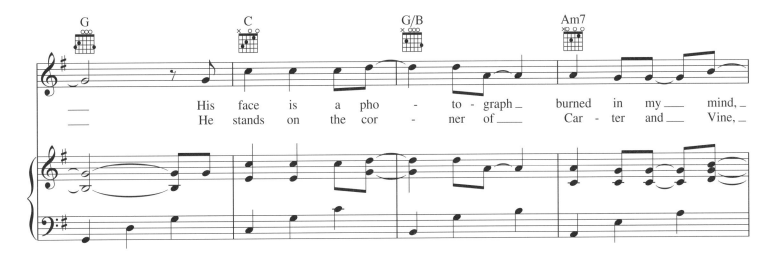

_____ His face is a pho - to - graph _____ burned in my _____ mind, _____
_____ He stands on the cor - ner of _____ Car - ter and _____ Vine, _____

_____ but I pre - tend not to see him for the twen - ty - first _____

time. _____ He

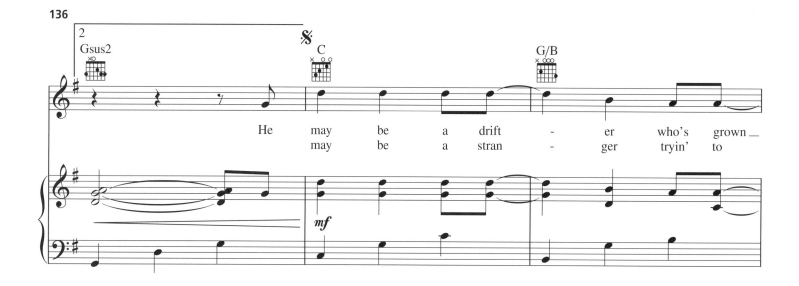

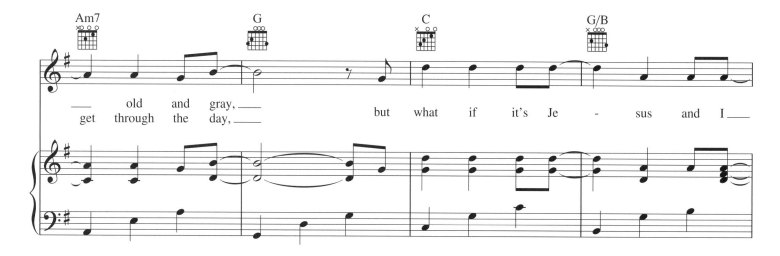

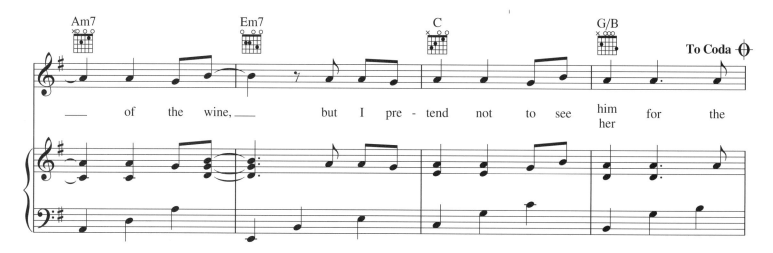

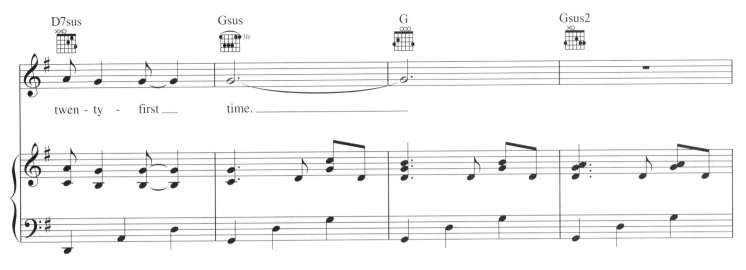

twen - ty - first ___ time. _____

She's twen - ty - nine, ___ but ___ she feels for - ty - eight. ___

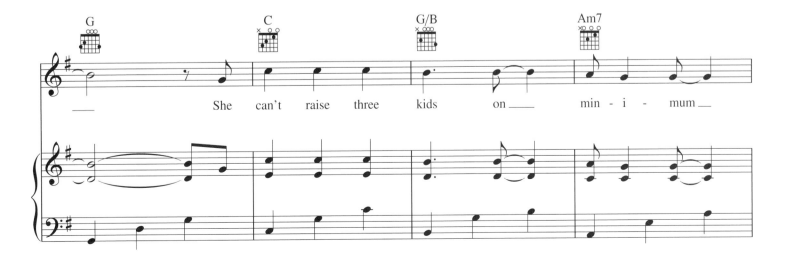

___ She can't raise three kids on ___ min - i - mum ___

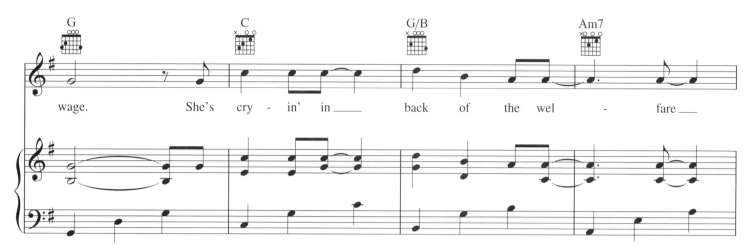

wage. She's cry - in' in ___ back of the wel - fare ___

line, but I pre - tend not to see her for the twen - ty - first ___

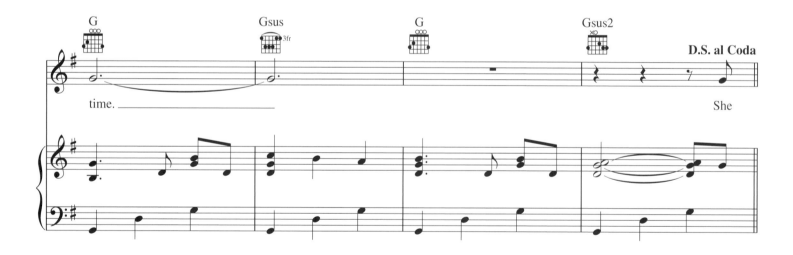

D.S. al Coda

time. ___ She

CODA

twen - ty - first ___ time. Yeah, ___

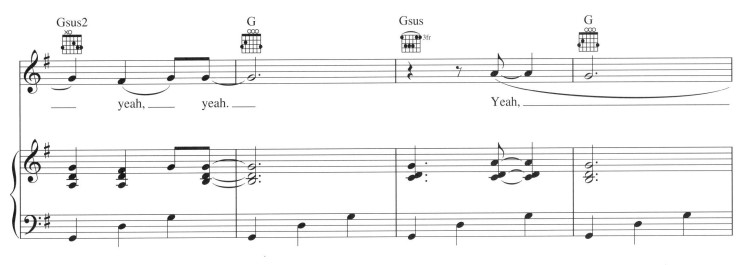

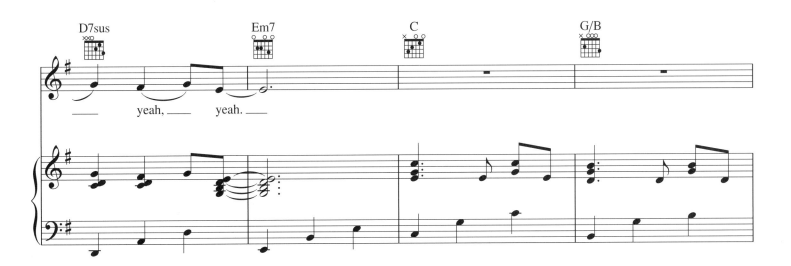

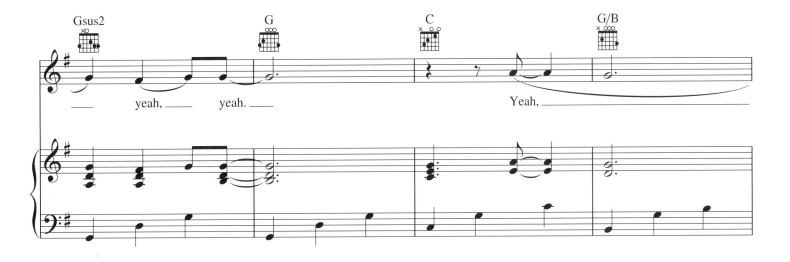

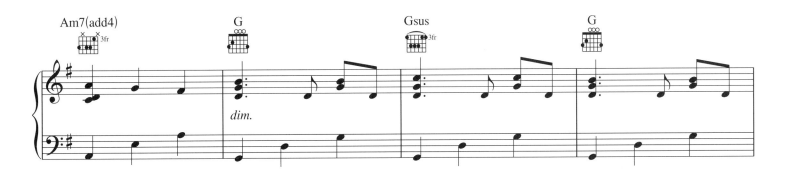

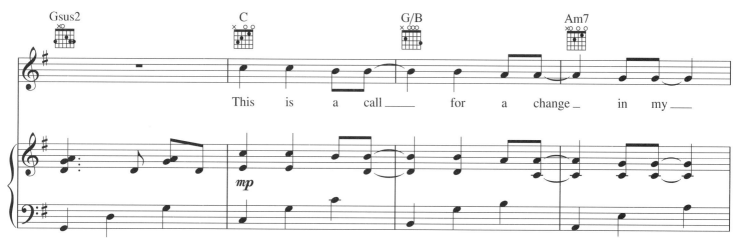

This is a call ___ for a change ___ in my ___

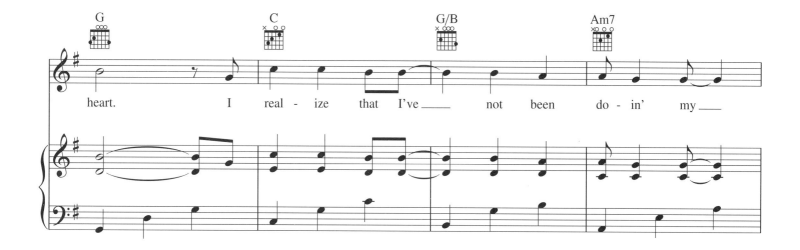

heart. I real - ize that I've ___ not been do - in' my ___

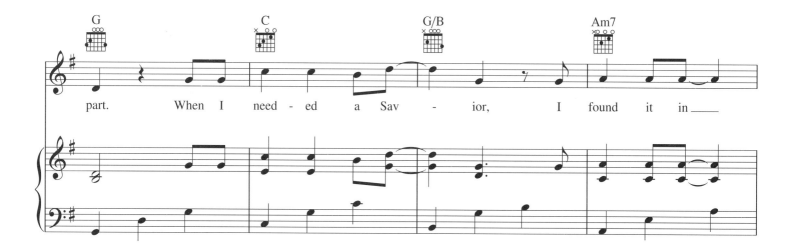

part. When I need - ed a Sav - ior, I found it in ___

Him. He gave to me, ___ now I'll ___ give back to them. ___

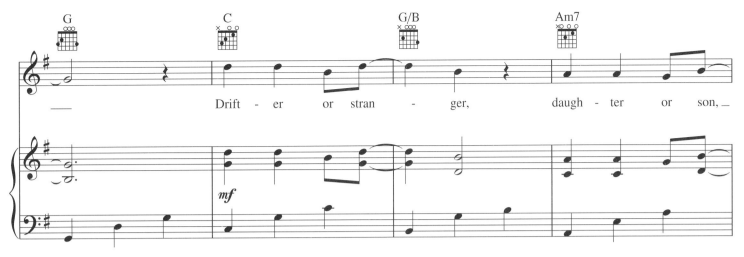

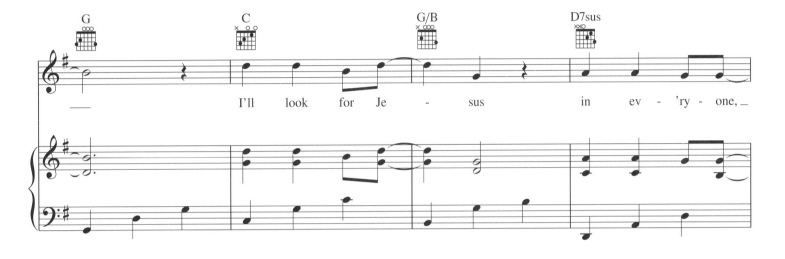

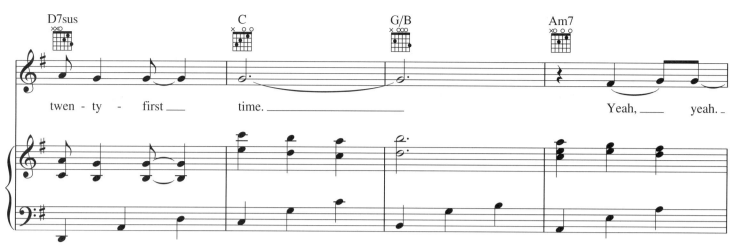

twen - ty - first ___ time. _____ Yeah, ___ yeah. _

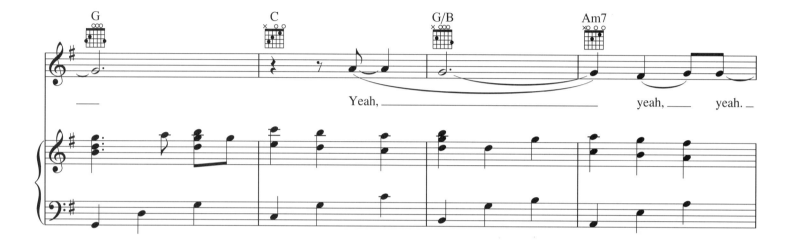

__ Yeah, _____ yeah, ___ yeah. _

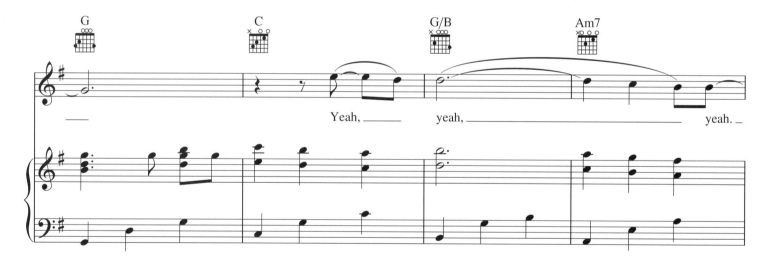

__ Yeah, ___ yeah, _____ yeah. _

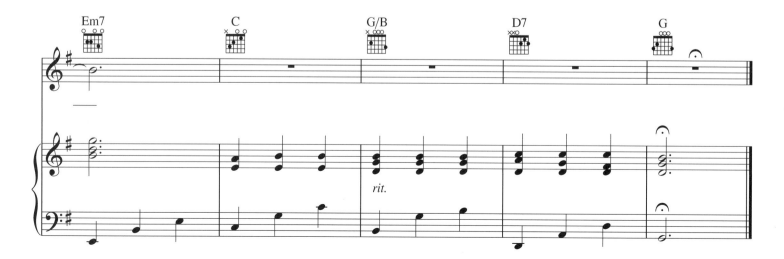

rit.